Roman Catholics in the qathet Region

The History of a Community

Baelena Books

Front Cover photograph:
View from Sacred Heart Catholic Church, Sliammon, 2012
Church of the Assumption Parish Archive

PUBLISHED BY BAELENA BOOKS
Powell River, BC Canada
baelena.mmerlino.com

Scripture texts in this work are taken from the New American Bible, revised edition © 2010, 1991, 1986, 1970 Confraternity of Christian Doctrine, Washington, D.C. and are used by permission of the copyright owner. All Rights Reserved. No part of the New American Bible may be reproduced in any form without permission in writing from the copyright owner.

Copyright © 2019 by Baelena Books
All rights reserved. No part of this publication may be reproduced without prior permission.
Legal Deposit: National Library of Canada, Ottawa

Merlino, Mark, author, 1979-
Roman Catholics in the qathet Region the History of a Community / Mark Merlino.

(qathet Regional District, Roman Catholic Church, history)
Includes bibliographical references.
Issued in print format.
ISBN: 978-0-9951731-4-9

1. Christianity History — Canada — qathet Regional District. 2. Catholic Church History, 1850s - Present.
I. Title.

TABLE OF CONTENTS

5	Acknowledgements
6	Foreword By Sister Claire Sapiano and Sister Rose Vella
7	Abbreviations
8	A Note on Orthography
9	Map
10	Part 1 — The Mission of Saint Charles
24	Part 2 — The Original Mission Churches
33	Part 3 — Saint Joseph's Parish
50	Part 4 — Church of the Assumption

APPENDICES

90	Archives Consulted
90	Individuals Consulted
90	Websites Consulted
91	Selected Primary Sources
92	Selected Secondary Sources
93	Oblate Missionaries
94	Saint Joseph's Pastors and Assistant Pastors
95	Assumption Church Pastors and Assistant Pastors

Acknowledgements

A project of writing the history of a community, spanning 160 years is an enormous undertaking. The word *qathet* means working together in the Tla'amin language and this idea has been an inspiration for me. A special sense of gratitude must be extended to Elio Cossarin, Betty Wilson, Professor Jacqueline Gresko, and Sister Claire Sapiano MSJN, without whose inspiration and assistance this project would not have been possible. I also wish to express my own profound sense of respect and appreciation to Les Adams, Beatrice Gaudet, Dr. Elsie Paul, Evelyn Rigby and Frank Rigby for supporting this project with their memories and guidance. I am deeply indebted to Bridget Bigold and Ann Waite for collecting a wealth of pictures and documents in the Church of the Assumption Archive.

I would like to express gratitude to my wife Barbara Fiorentino for listening to my stories, editing the manuscript and supporting me as I researched and wrote over the past few years.

I extend my deepest appreciation to each of the following people for their inspiration, gracious assistance in guiding me and assisting me answering my queries.

Brad Adams, Leslie Adams, Gerry Bennett, Bev Bernard, Bridget Bigold, Veronica Bourassa, Charlene and Don Bourcier, Father John Brioux OMI, Stephen Cantryn, Patricia Clark, Father Terry Conway OMI, Elio Cossarin, Father Dass, Father Glenn Dion, Barbara Fiorentino, Beatrice Gaudet, Professor Jacqueline Gresko, Father Bruce-John Hamilton, Mary Harry, Denise Jablonsky, Verna Lentz, Elena Merlino, Dr. Elsie Paul, Theresa Pinel, Mimi Richardson, Evelyn and Frank Rigby, Sister Claire Sapiano MSJN, Jennifer Sargent, Frances Schweitzer, Theresa Slack, Rose Ann Sole, Father Patrick Tepoorten, Mary Lou Vella, Sister Rose Vella MSJN, Ann Waite, Diane Wardle, Betty Wilson and Sharon Wright.

Mark Merlino
Powell River
January 28, 2019

The works of all mankind are present to Him
  Not a thing escapes his eye.
  His gaze spans all the ages.

The Book of Sirach 39:19-20

Foreword

Sister Rose Vella and I, Sister Claire, had the pleasure to read the book *Roman Catholics in the qathet Region the History of a Community*. This book is easy to read, full of details, photos and it gives a good description of how the first Missionaries brought the Catholic Faith to the First Nations on the Sunshine Coast. Later on when the Mill started operating many immigrants came to Powell River and there was the need to built St. Joseph's Church and rectory.

When you think of all the sacrifices and the hardships that the first Missionaries went through to bring the Catholic Faith and the Sacraments and how the First Nations welcomed them, it made us ask the question, "Do we thank God enough for the Faith that was given to us from our forefathers?" It will be nice if everyone will get a chance to read it. Thank you Mr. Merlino for all the hard work you did to write this book.

Sister Claire Sapiano and Sister Rose Vella
Żejtun, Malta, June 29, 2018

Abbreviations

AoV— Archdiocese of Vancouver
BCA— British Columbia Archives
BCC— The BC Catholic Paper
CoA— Church of the Assumption Parish Archives
CRS— Canada's Residential Schools: The History Part 1 Origins to 1939
IA— Department of Indian Affairs, Canada Archives
IR— Indian Record
KW— Kamloops Wawa
MCMOMI—Missions de la Congrégation des missionnaires oblats de Marie Immaculée
NM— NehMotl Newsletter
PRDS—Powell River & District Schools
OMI— Oblates of Immaculate Mary
SLSL— Sliammon Life Sliammon Lands
WaIR— Written As I Remember It

A Note on Orthography

Wherever possible, an effort has been made to include Tla'amin words and place names for the Tla'amin, Klahoose and Homalco First Nations using the International Phonetic Alphabet Orthography as it is used by the Tla'amin Nation.

I have found the First Voices website: **www.firstvoices.com** to be a great resource to learn about the ɬəʔamɛn language, its orthography and access a pronunciation guide. I would like to acknowledge the tireless effort of Betty Wilson in preserving this invaluable linguistic heritage and I would like to thank her personally for the advice that she has given me on Tla'amin orthography.

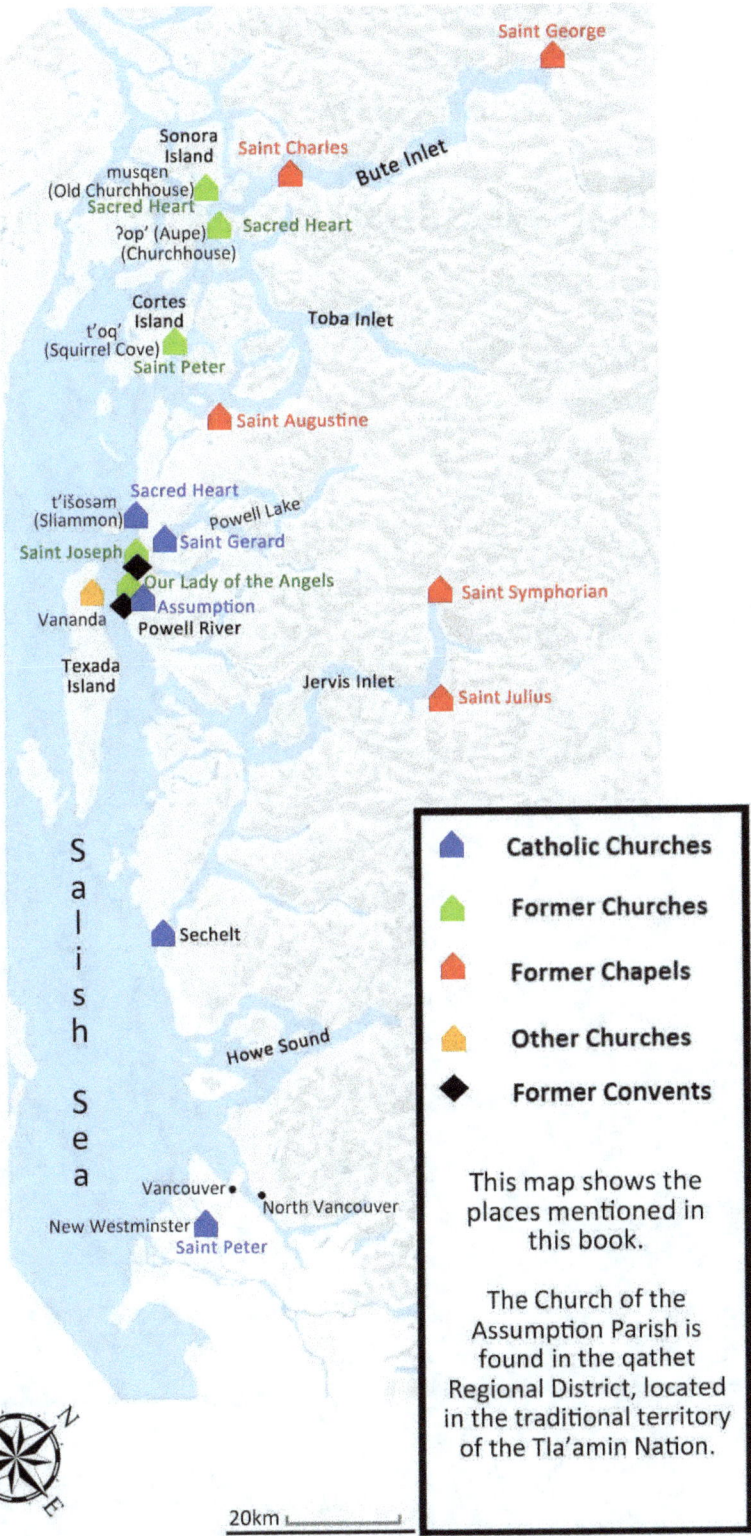

The Mission of Saint Charles

The first Catholic priests to minister to the territories of Assumption Parish were the Oblate Missionaries of Mary Immaculate who arrived in British Columbia in the 1850s. The original Oblate missionaries in the area were from France and they ministered to the First Nations in their native languages and in Chinook, which was the common language at the time. These priests came in high regard in BC for their tireless efforts in response to the smallpox pandemic of 1863, when they spearheaded a vaccination campaign and vaccinated thousands of First Nations in the province.

In 1860, Father Eugene Casimir Chirouse OMI and Leo Fouquet OMI became the first Catholic priests to visit the vicinity when they were hosted by the K'omoks First Nation on Vancouver Island.

In Nanaimo in 1860, Father Chirouse met three K'ómoks men, including the chief's son Noukinechass, who were eager to bring the priests to their land. Together en route the four men composed some prayers and hymns in the K'ómoks language, translating from Chinook and English. In the K'ómoks camp, Noukinechass and his father assembled everyone on the beach and they had a receiving ceremony where they touched hands with Father Fouquet and Father Chirouse, who then introduced who they were.

The priests then spent some days among the K'ómoks teaching the prayers and hymns that they had composed earlier, offering religious instruction and warning about alcohol that was spreading from nearby Nanaimo. Before leaving, the K'ómoks chief offered to lead them by canoe to the Yuculta on Quadra Island to the north with seven good rowers.

(MCMOMI Vol 3, P.174-179)

A young Father Eugene Casimir Chirouse, OMI. (OMI Archives)

The Missionary Oblates of Mary Immaculate were founded in 1816 in France by Saint Charles Joseph Eugene de Mazenod.

It is an order of priests and religious brothers dedicated to reviving the spirit of faith among industrial and rural populations and serving the poor.

The first recorded visit by a Catholic priest to the territory of the Tla'Amin, (ɬaʔəmen), and Klahoose, (λaʔos), First Nations was the visit by Father Leon Fouquet OMI in January 1868.

Father Fouquet was heading to Saint Michael's mission post on Harbledown Island (est. 1864), east of Alert Bay, and left New Westminster by canoe on December 30, 1867 with a Shishalh (Sechelt) man who was returning home. He then visited the Shishalh communities for some time before being accompanied by canoe to the village of tišosəm, Teeshohsum, at Sliammon Creek. They came in sight of the village at night and fired a rifle in the air to announce their arrival. The people of tišosəm, including the Klahoose who were wintering there, lined up to greet Father Fouquet whom they called *laplɛt* from the French *le prêtre* for priest. Father Fouquet spent Saturday evening and all of Sunday with the people. He visited and spoke with each of the families, baptized several children and heard many confessions. He also prayed with the community and spent time instructing in the catechism. He was unable to celebrate mass however, as he had not brought a portable altar with him.

Father Leon Fourquet, OMI.
(Late 19th c. OMI Archives)

On Monday, the people of tišosəm escorted Father Fouquet by canoe to another Tla'amin camp. As they paddled they sung Tla'amin canoe hymns until they were overcome by a gust of snow. The people in the camp were very surprised to see a priest arrive by canoe in such icy water.

One man named Peter was overjoyed, and asked Father Fouquet to hear his confession, saying that it was just too far to travel all the way to New Westminster. The Tla'amin chief and Peter convinced Father Fouquet to remain an extra day with them there.

They then escorted him in a large canoe that could hand the winter weather to the Yaculta on Quadra Island. There, the Tla'amin assisted Father Fouquet in translating and teaching some prayers and hymns to the Yaculta in their language before saying goodbye and heading home, while he continued on to Saint Michaels.

(MCMOMI Vol. 9, P.122, 127-128)

Catholic priests first visited the territories of the Tla'Amin (ɫaʔəmen), Klahoose (ƛaʔos) and Homalco (χoχmałku) First Nations during the 1860s but did not establish permanent chapels in these lands. Many First Nations actually first encountered the Catholic Church in New Westminster at Saint Peter's Church, built in 1860 as the headquarters to the Oblates mission on the coast. In order to receive sacraments, the baptized would occasionally make the long trip by canoe to Saint Peter's Church in New Westminster.

In July of 1870, Father Paul Durieu OMI made for the first time what would become the standard route for the priest's visit to the Sunshine Coast, including visits to Sechelt, the Tla Amin Nation and then reaching the communities along Bute Inlet.

(MCMOMI Vol. 9, Pages 386-393)

Canoe on the Homathko River, at the head of Bute Inlet.
(1875, BC Archives)

During the 1870s, Oblate missionaries, Father Paul Durieu OMI, Father Le Jack OMI and Father Marchal OMI continued to visit the Tla'Amin, Klahoose and Homalco First Nations. The oblate fathers sought to visit these communities for missions once a year, usually in the winter time. It was at this time that oratories or chapels were established in the communities that they served. On one such visit in the year 1872 Father Marchal reached an agreement with chiefs from the Tla'Amin and Klahoose Nations that a new church needed to be built at tišosəm so that it would be large enough to hold all of the congregations. The Sacred Heart of Jesus chapel was established at the site of the present Sacred Heart church and it was dedicated in 1873. A chapel dedicated to Saint Augustine was set up on Toba Inlet and two chapels, Saint Charles and Saint George, were dedicated on Bute Inlet.

(MCMOMI Vol. 11-12, p. 322)

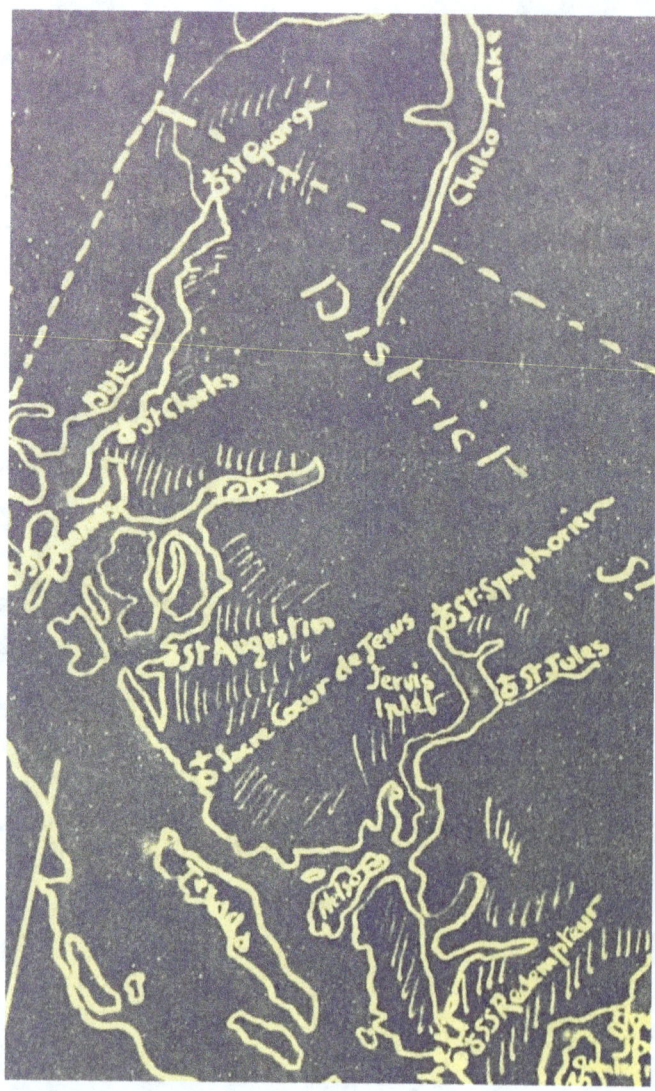

Map of what is now Assumption Catholic Parish in circa 1890.
(c. 1890, AoV Archives)

Father Eugene Chirouse OMI the younger, who was the nephew of the other Eugene Casimir Chirouse OMI, known affectionately as *Father Chaleuse*, came to BC and was assigned the duty of being regular missionary to the Tla'Amin, Klahoose and Homalco Nations. He arrived in New Westminster from France in October 1879 with fellow Oblate Jean-Marie-Raphaël Le Jeune and then served the mission on the coast from 1880 until 1926. He made three visits each year to each community travelling by canoe guided by rowers from each congregation and also led the congregations in participating in the large religious mission gatherings in different cities in British Columbia.

Father Chirouse was a skilled linguist and he regularly preached in numerous First Nations languages, including Chinook and the Tla'amin language. During his visits, he would follow a set routine, involving teaching the catechism, hearing confessions and visiting those who were sick.

The younger Fr Eugene Casimir Chirouse, OMI. (early 20th c., BC Archives)

The cemetery in tišosəm was first dedicated and blessed in 1878 and was located north of the church next to the current cemetery. An expansion of the cemetery was blessed by Archbishop J. Michael Miller and Father Edwin Neufeld in 2012.

Archbishop Michael Miller blessing the cemetery. (2012, CoA)

Oblate missionaries, following the example of Father Paul Durieu OMI, promoted a system of organization for each congregation that was adapted to a small community with infrequent priestly visits. In 1888, Land Commissioner Peter O'Reilly described tišosəm as consisting of a large Catholic Church, 47 houses and 317 inhabitants. In each community, a notable person was appointed as Watchman by the priest. The Watchman functioned as a sacristan and truant officer. He would keep an eye on the community, lead prayer services in the absence of a priest and would bring the congregation together when the priest was visiting. As well, a bell man rang the church bell for prayers and mass and there was a Captain, who organized and maintained the upkeep of the church building.

During mission gatherings that the community attended in other cities, the Watchman or another member of the congregation would repeat sermons in ʔayʔajuθəm, Ayajuthem, the Tla'amin language, since the priest was preaching in Chinook. The Watchman would elaborate on the meaning for the congregation, while translating.

(MCMOMI Vol. 33-34, p. 473; NM March, 2018, p.6)

Bishop Paul Durieu OMI.
(mid 19th c. AoV Archives)

Gathering of First nations for a passion play on Good Friday, 1901 in Sechelt.
(1901, Sechelt Municipal Archive)

Bishop d'Herbomez OMI of New Westminster, the first Catholic bishop in this territory, developed a personal connection with the Tla'amin nation. In the late 1870s, d'Herbomez assisted several Tla'amin in sending letters to the Indian Land Commissioner Gilbert Sproat with concerns about white settlers arriving in their territory without permits to settle and requesting the protection of Tla'amin lands through a land survey. D'Herbomez then became the first bishop to make a pastoral visit to the territory when he came in 1884 to confirm many catechumens. The following is the Bishop d'Herbomz's description of what he beheld on his return journey to Sechelt accompanied by Father Chirouse and Tla'amin rowers in the Watchman's grand canoe the *Yougoulia*:

"We entered a sort of labyrinth formed by numerous islands of various sizes, between which the wind was hardly felt. This forced detour lengthened our trip, but we far from regretted it. Our eyes admired the beautiful spectacle which nature offers the astonished traveler in this place. The sea is infinitely divided and subdivided into groups of extremely picturesque islands all the way to the hilltops on the continent, forming a backdrop of virgin forest covered peaks of 200 or 300 feet in height."

(MCMOMI Vol. 22, p. 415-416, 419; NM Feb, 2018 p.1)

Bishop d'Herbomez
(late 19th c., AoV)

Texada and Vancouver Island from Powell River, 2016.

During the 1880s and 1890s, Catholics from the First Nations on the Sunshine Coast travelled to other communities for annual Mission gatherings. These festive occasions took place in Sechelt, North Vancouver and Kamloops and brought together First Nations from throughout British Columbia. At the missions, the priest would preach in the Chinook language and then lay members from each Nation would translate what was being said into their own tongue.

The Canadian Pacific Railway kindly offered free transportation on one occasion for a very large mission gathering in Kamloops in 1892. Father Chirouse attended this gathering accompanied by the faithful from the Tla'Amin Nation, as well as others from Sechelt and Squamish. Rose Mitchell remembered years later that Tla'Amin women learned different cedar root basketry techniques from other First Nations they met at such prayer gathering in Kamloops, which lead this period to the highpoint of Tla'Amin basketry.

(MCMOMI Vol. 31-32, p. 129-131; SLSL 76; WaIR 396)

Gathering of the First Nations at an outdoor altar for Easter or Corpus Christi at Sechelt. (c. 1900., Sechelt Municipal Archives)

Father Chirouse's description of the mission gathering on Burrard Inlet for the feast of Corpus Christi June 14, 1886.

"The Seashels preserved the honor of carrying the statue of the Sacred Heart, placed on an artistically decorated stretcher. The Skromishs formed a beautiful procession to Our Lady of Lourdes. The Tlayamine were at the head of the procession, leading the way carrying the statue of Saint Joseph.

At the canon volley, all of the houses lit up as if by magic. All of these dear Indians advanced forth in admirable order with candles in hand. They celebrated with joyful songs and pious praise for Jesus, Mary, and Joseph.

Calm weather and overcast skies made it possible to behold and enjoy the brilliance projected by this line of lights gracefully curving along the sea and on the edge of the forest. The Bishop in pontifical vestments, was at the end of this triumphant march. The whites who were there grouped along the route of the procession, holding their hats, contemplating this edifying religious spectacle. We arrived at the main altar. It was a throne of lights erected in honor of the Holy Family. Each statue was placed in its respective place with the Sacred Heart in the middle. Kneeling before it, the Seashels tribe sung the hymn of the Guard of Honour, followed by a touching prayer showing their devotion to this adorable Heart. A flare was lit at that time shining its light on the statue of the Sacred Heart and the whole assembly in its magical glow.

The Skromish in turn worshipped before Our Lady of Lourdes, expressing their gratitude and love in touching terms. A second flare was lit shining upon it. Finally, the Tlayamine sang the glory of Saint Joseph, and followed that with their prayer song: 'Remember.' A third flare shone forth on the statue of our patron saint. "

(MCMOMI Vol. 24-25, P. 470-471)

(Sunshine Coast Museum and Archives, 1927)

In the 1890s, the arrival of regular steamship service to the Sunshine Coast from the city of Vancouver drastically changed life on the coast. Travel to the city had become easy and quick and this allowed for an influx of newcomers into the territory. The SS Catala (above) made regular stops at the city of Powell River in the early twentieth century. The journey by ship from Vancouver to tišosəm took about five hours, while Squirrel Cove was an additional three hours north and Church House about another three hours further north from there.

Sechelt District, 1957. BCA #A00826..29.14

Father Jean-Raphael Le Jeune OMI, who was an excellent linguist and publisher of the Chinook language Catholic newspaper the *Kamloops Wawa*. He also published prayer books in Chinook and these were in use among the Tla'Amin Nation. Chinook hymns were sung for many years at Sacred Heart. On one Mission in Sechelt in 1896, Fr. Le Jeune transcribed many prayers and readings into the Tla'Amin language. Unfortunately, it does not appear that a copy of the Tla'amin language prayer book work survived to the present day. One such Tla'amin translator was Molly Timothy, Elsie Paul's grandmother, who was skilled in languages and translated Chinook prayers and homilies into the Tla'amin language. Traditional Tla'Amin Catholic devotional songs, such as *Oh Mahleh* (O Blessed Mary), are noted for their beauty and are still sung in Sacred Heart Church to this day.

(MCMOMI. Vol. 33-34, p. 467, 471-474; WaIR p. 392, 396)

Prayers Hymns and Catechism in Chinook published by Father Le Jeune, OMI in 1896.

ʔo ʔii malɛ — *Oh Blessed Mary*
Traditional Tla'amin Hymn Sung at Mass
(Courtesy of Betty Wilson)

ʔo ʔi malɛ
Oh blessed Mary

nɪgi ʔəms tan
You are our mother

ʔi kʷaθ kʷaʔətumoɬ
Have mercy on us

ʔo ʔi malɛ
Oh blessed Mary

nɪgi ʔəms tan
You are our mother

ʔəms χaƛ kʷums kʷʊnomɛ nɪgi
We would very much like to see you

kʷums hoysam ʔa te gɪjɛ
When we leave this earth

ʔi kʷaθ kʷaʔətumoɬaxʷ
Have mercy on us

ʔo ʔɛʔɛy malɛ
Oh blessed Mary

(Repeats Three Times)

Traditional Tla'amin Christmas Hymn Sung Before Mass
(Courtesy of Betty Wilson)

ʔɛʔanə manəs šišɛƛɛ
Born the child of the Lord

ʔɛʔanə čʊy šišɛƛɛ
Birth of baby Jesus

(Repeats Three Times)

Indian Day Schools were established as local elementary schools at Church House (1908) and on the Sliammon Reserve (1914). The Day School at the Sliammon Reserve included some Catholic religious instruction and it operated until 1961. The Indian agent who recruited teachers to work at the Day Schools tried to find lay men and women, who shared the same Catholic faith of the communities they would serve. The schools were occasionally staffed by retired school teachers, such as Mr. and Mrs. Gallagher who taught at the Sliammon and Church House Day Schools from 1948 to 1958. After the Sliammon Day School's closure in 1961, students began to attend other local schools in Powell River.

The Saint Augustine's Indian Residential School was set up in Sechelt (1912-1975), operated by the oblate missionaries and the sisters of the Child Jesus. It functioned as a residential elementary school for First Nations children not attending the Day Schools or for those from communities without local schools. Residential high schools were operated by the oblates and sisters of Saint Anne in Mission and in Kamloops starting in the 1940s and other students also attended high school in Sechelt and North Vancouver.

The Canadian government made Residential School attendance compulsory for First Nations in 1920. Residential schools involved the forcible and traumatic separation of children from their parents and were noted for being very strict. For instance Tla'amin child Lily Francis (b.1905) attended Residential School in Sechelt until she was 16 and, as was the rule in such schools, she was not allowed to use her own Tla'amin language during the school year. Many students dropped out of attending Residential Schools as soon as they could. This system resulted in discontinuity within families, considerable cultural loss and instances of abuse within the schools. Compulsory attendance in Residential Schools for First Nations officially ended in 1948, though families were coerced into sending their children to such schools in the following decades until the remaining Indian Residential schools were finally closed.

(CRS—p. 279; IA c-8736-01514; IR February 1956 – Vol 21 N. 2, p.6; PRDS p. 10; WaIR p. 90-91, 184-186, 196-197)

Sliammon Day School in 1918 with the teacher Mr. Nicholson (fourth from left)
Father Brabander from Sechelt (fifth from the right)
and Captain Timothy (fourth from the right). (1918, BC Archives)

Apology to First Nations by the Archbishop of Vancouver

"I wish to repeat once again the Archdiocese's sincere and heartfelt apology for the role that the Church played in the federal government's policy which involved forcibly separating children from their families and placing them in residential schools. Likewise, I acknowledge our error in supporting a policy that aimed at suppressing Aboriginal cultures and language. This federal policy contributed to the pain and suffering experienced by generations of First Nations children and adults…. We will continue to seeks ways to contribute to healing and education in the Archdiocese of Vancouver, and to teach the full truth about the history about the encounter between Aboriginal and non-Aboriginal peoples."

(Archbishop Michael Miller, Formal Apology to First Nations, 2015)

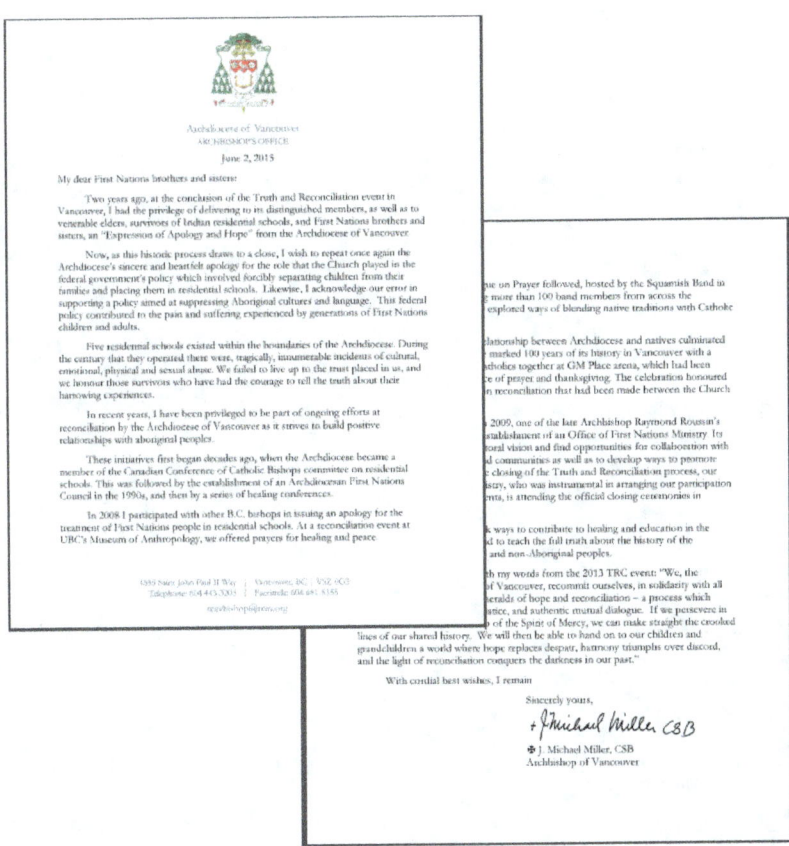

Letter of Apology by Archbishop Michael Miller of Vancouver to First Nations of the Archdiocese on Residential Schools. (2015, AoV)

The Original Mission Churches

In the 1890s, construction of large permanent churches was undertaken. Sacred Heart Church was built at t̓išosəm, Saint Peter's Church was built at toq̓ or Squirrel Cove on Cortes Island and Sacred Heart Church was built at musqɛn (Muushkin) or Old Church House on Sonora Island. At the beginning of the 1900s, Sacred Heart Church at Old Church House on Sonora Island was hit by a hurricane force winds coming down Bute Inlet, likely in excess of 150 knots, that tore the steeple off of the church and blew it far behind the village. After this, the village was relocated after that terrible storm to Church House, where a new church was built.

The Catholic Church on Cortes Island was dedicated as Saint Peter's Church. It was built on Cortes Island in 1896 with wood that was logged by the Klahoose First Nation on Toba Inlet and was then towed to Washington State to be milled.

(Swan, A. *House Calls Float Plane*. p.89)

Saint Peter's Church with its original steeple, toq̓, Squirrel Cove, Cortes Island.
(c.1910s, Cortes Island Museum and Archive)

The bell tower on Saint Peter's Church (mistakenly identified as Saint Michael's Church in recent years) was rebuilt in the 1920s because it was unable to support the great weight of the bell. The Church bell was rung in order to announce to the community the arrival of visitors or the death of someone from the community. The original church building was demolished in 2018, after it was determined to be in unstable condition and having been in disuse for nearly forty years.

Each of the mission churches included a small room next to the main church that the priest would use both as a sacristy and as a room to sleep during his stay in the community.

Saint Peter's Church after renovations and its modified steeple,
toq̓, Squirrel Cove, Cortes Island.
(c.1929, Cortes Island Museum and Archive)

In 1898, Tla'Amin leader Captain Timothy obtained permits to built a new large Sacred Heart Church to replace the existing one that had a rotten sagging floor. Tla'amin loggers cut, hauled and milled the wood for the church using traditional methods. The enlarged brand new church was formally dedicated on October 8, 1901 and was noted for its beauty and was decorated with a metallic ceiling on the inside. The church was blessed by Bishop Dontenwill of New Westminster, who celebrated the first mass there. The bishop arrived from Vancouver by steam ship and was accompanied by Fathers Chirouse, Le Jeune, Tavernier and Bellot.

The previous smaller Sacred Heart Church was kept to be used for a meeting room and Catechism house.

The Tla'amin community purchased a large bell in the 1880s from San Francisco for the original Sacred Heart Church. The ringing of the bell at Sacred Heart Church has always been a way to inform the community of someone's death. When a child dies, the bell is rung slowly seven times. Eight bell tolls indicate a woman died and nine bell tolls indicate a man died.

(KW Vol.10 N.4, Dec. 1901; NM Apr. 2018, p.1,5; Osmond, C. "Giant Trees." p.32-34)

The First Sacred Heart Church, Sliammon. (c.1914, CoA)

Sadly, tišosəm was destroyed by the great fire of 1918. In that terrible fire, both the original church and the new larger church were burned to the ground.
Remarkably the statue of the Sacred Heart of Jesus was left undamaged. This statue stands today above the main entrance of the current Sacred Heart Catholic Church.

The Sacred Heart of Jesus statue in Sacred Heart Church after the great fire of 1918.
(1918, CoA)

Sarah *qʷoqʷʔasukt* Adams

Sarah *qʷoqʷʔasukt* Adams was born in Sliammon in 1880 and was one of five children. Her grandfather Tlesla was one of the last great Tla'amin warriors. Tlelsa was a skilled hunter and a good shot with a rifle and fought against other warriors at Harwood Island.

Growing up, Sarah learned to speak the Tla'amin language, which she spoke in the community, Chinook and English, both of which she used to talk to those from other places, and some Latin, which was used in church. As a girl she learned many skills and knew how to shoot a gun. She got married and had eight children and worked hard to provide for her family, travelling at night to dig and smoke clams and spending her summers in Washington State harvesting berries and hops. She ran her household on her own after her husband became sick and later died in the Lower Mainland. She became the matriarch of the family, advising all of her daughters and their spouses.

Sarah did considerable service in the community and was a leader in the church. She was the local midwife and offered her service without being paid and would also assist in preparing for the burials whenever someone died. Sarah served as a catechist, preparing children for their First Holy Communions and Confirmations and was talented in singing hymns, which were sung in the Tla'amin, Chinook and Latin.

Sarah is fondly remembered as *hays qaymɪχʷ*, a most respected elder, and was a source of inspiration to her family. She raised her grandson Les Adams after his mother died of tuberculosis when he was a baby. She taught Les to fear no man and no animal, never to give away something that you do not yourself cherish and that there was no such thing as, 'I can't do it.' Les followed her inspiration to go on to become chief at age 26, her example for how to raise children and her advice in his professional life. Sarah Adams died in 1963 at age 83.

Sarah Adams
in 1953 in Sliammon
(Courtesy of Les Adams)

A new Catholic Church dedicated to the Sacred Heart of Jesus was built by the Homalco First Nation at Church House (ʔop̓) and it was consecrated c. 1917. There was a small room built on the side of the church where the priest would stay during his visit to the community and it also had a fireplace for heat. This church was noted for its beauty and held a statue of Christ with his Sacred Heart and arms open wide above the main entrance.

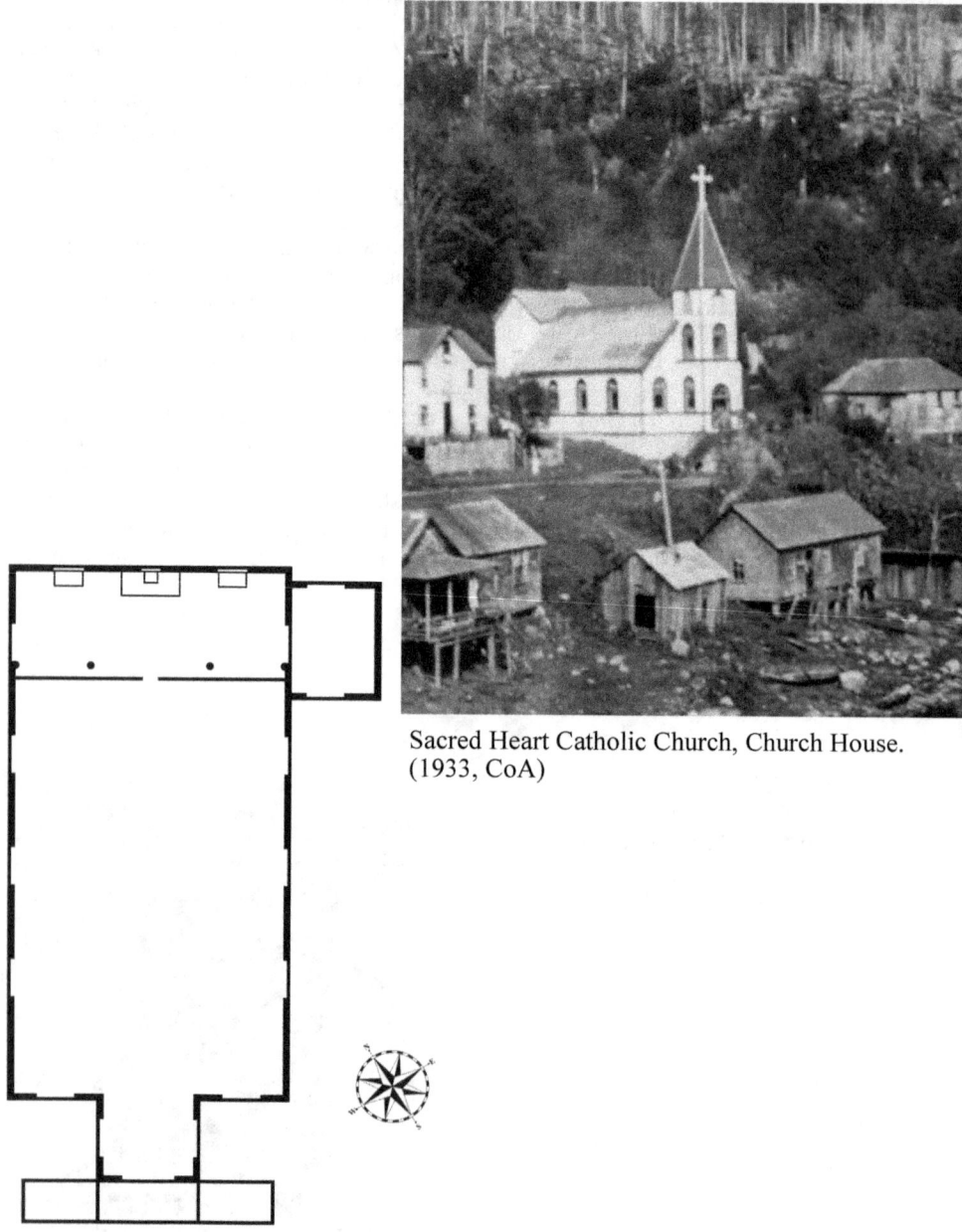

Sacred Heart Catholic Church, Church House. (1933, CoA)

Floor Plan for Sacred Heart Catholic Church, Church House. (Reconstruction)

The present Sacred Heart Church in tišosəm was built immediately after the great fire of 1918. The wood for the church was logged and milled by the Tla'Amin using logs that had been scorched by the great fire.

Jim Rae helps with transporting the statue of the Sacred Heart of Jesus during the restoration of Sacred Heart Church. (2012, CoA)

Devotion to the Sacred Heart of Jesus began in 17th c. France , following apparitions to mystic Saint Margaret Mary Alacoque. The devotion became universal in the 1880s with the mystical revelations of Blessed Mary of the Divine Heart, inspiring Pope Leo XIII to dedicate the entire world to the Sacred Heart of Jesus in 1899.

The oblate order has always promoted a strong devotion to the Sacred Heart of Jesus, following the example of Saint Eugene de Mazenod.

The current Sacred Heart Catholic Church, Sliammon. (early 20th c., CoA)

Interior of Sacred Heart Catholic Church, Sliammon.
(2001, CoA)

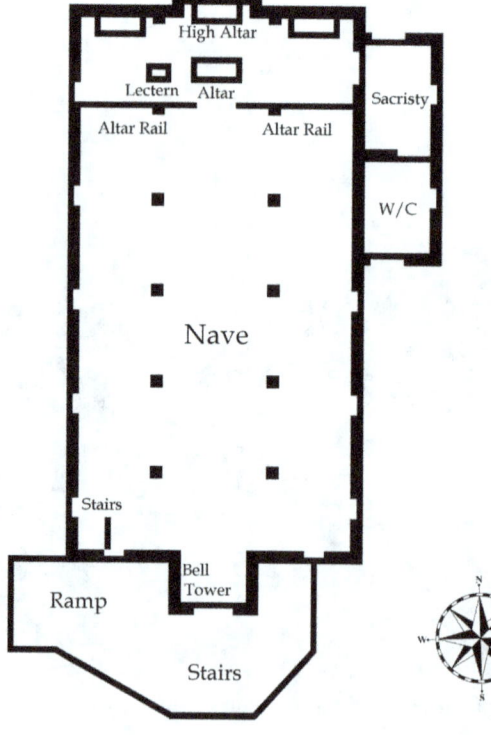

Floor Plan for Sacred Heart Catholic Church, Sliammon. (Reconstruction)

Saint Joseph's Parish

The Powell River Company began construction of a pulp and paper mill town, now called Townsite, at the mouth of Powell River in 1910. Many Catholic immigrants were among the newcomers who arrived there to work in the mill. In 1915, a temporary cafeteria was transformed into a Catholic Church and the first pastor Fr. Bonner served the community on a coast mission before the Mill built the original saint Joseph's in 1915. The coast mission priest only occasionally visited the community and Catholics from Powell River also traveled to Sacred Heart in Sliammon to receive the sacraments.

Original Saint Joseph's Catholic Church, Townsite, Powell River.
(In use from 1911-1916, Church of the Assumption Parish Archives)

First Catholic boys choir at Saint Joseph's Catholic Church.
(1911, Powell River Municipal Archives)

The growing congregation saved money to build a new Catholic Church and construction started in 1916. The second Saint Joseph's became the centre of the new Saint Joseph's Catholic Parish of Powell River. From the earliest days, many of the members of the parish were Italian immigrants who had come to work in the mill.

It seemed fitting that the new parish in a new mill town was dedicated to Saint Joseph, the protector of workers. In fact, in this period Archbishop of Vancouver Neil McNeil dedicated four new parishes in the Archdiocese to Saint Joseph, who was named patron of the universal church and patron of workers in 1889. In 1912, the same Archbishop wrote a pastoral letter for Labour Day promoting the dignity of labour, as outlined by Pope Leo XIII's Encyclical *Rerum Novarum* from 1891.

At the time when there was only one Catholic Church in the mill town of Powell River, parishioners from Wildwood, Cranberry and Westview would either walk, take the bus or drive down to Saint Joseph's to attend mass.

Father Van Wetten in front of the new Saint Joseph's Catholic Church, Townsite.
(1923, Powell River Municipal Archives)

Saint Joseph's Catholic Church, Christmas, 1921. (1921, CoA)
On Christmas Eve there used to be large dances held in Dwight Hall, next to the mill. Many parishioners would leave the Christmas dances to attend midnight mass at St Joseph's then would head back down the hill to Dwight Hall and dance late into Christmas morning.

Father Van Wetten and the First Communion Class. (1920s, CoA)

During the late 1930s, Fr. Leo Hobson was a young dynamic priest built up St Joseph's parish, establishing a chapter of the Catholic Women's League in 1935 and then building a rectory and the Our Lady of Good Counsel parish hall in 1937. Fr. Hobson is fondly remembered as a true priest and a fabulous speaker who brought the parish to life in both the social and spiritual realms. The new hall he built became home to the kindergarten and following the advice of Archbishop Duke, he invited three sisters from the Sisters of Charity of the Immaculate Conception to come to the parish. His hope was that the Kindergarten would become the first step to opening a parish school in Powell River. This Kindergarten was attended by children of all communities in Townsite, Catholic and non-Catholic alike, since there was no other Kindergarten in town at the time. The sisters' house in town was called Saint Joseph's Convent.

The first Sisters to arrive were Sister Catherina Murphy, Superior and an experienced primary teacher for the Kindergarten class, Sister Celine-Evelyn Goodine to teach piano and music and Sister Paula Power for catechetical work. Saint Joseph's Convent was located in different houses in Townsite, first on Maple Avenue and later on Poplar Ave. The sisters also were very active getting out into the community to teach Catechism in Cranberry, Wildwood and Westview, as well as teaching catechism at Saint Joseph's and supporting the CWL activities in Townsite. In Cranberry, they held Catechism in the Gaudet house every Wednesday afternoon for the roughly twenty Catholic children from that neighbourhood.

The Second Saint Joseph's Convent in Townsite Powell River. (1952, CoA)

Saint Joseph's Kindergarten was located upstairs in the Our Lady of Good Counsel Hall. The class was very full with over fifty students enrolled, over half of whom were not Catholics, while the music classes that were also taught by the sisters had about eight pupils.

Kindergarten student Marne Bernard (left).

Class photo with both Saint Joseph's Kindergarten classes. Sister Carmelita (left) and very kind piano teacher Sister Imelda (right). (1954, CoA)

Father Hobson's mother Mrs. Edith Hobson arrived in Powell River with him in 1935. Together they set up the Catholic women's league in Saint Joseph's parish, holding their first meeting on November 17, 1935. The CWL did hospital visits, altar work, raised funds for the parish by the Telephone Bridge and Weekly Teas that supported the parish hall building project. They also run home cooking sales, a parish bazaar and gave away Christmas hampers.

The Catholic Women's League of Canada is a national organization rooted in gospel values calling its members to holiness through service to the people of God. The objects of the League shall be to unite Catholic women of Canada.

During World War Two, despite rationing, the CWL continued with its bake sales and bazaar to raise funds for the parish. The CWL also joined the red cross in sewing bedpan covers, hospital and surgical gowns and knitting socks to support the war effort.

Saint Joseph's Parish Picnic in 1950. (1950, CoA)

Sister Mary Bertrand SCIC

Sister Mary Bertrand (Margaret Dunn) was born in Saint John New Brunswick in 1923 and she was a gifted singer. After entering the Sisters of Charity of the Immaculate Conception in 1939 at the age of seventeen, she asked to be sent to Saint Joseph's parish in Powell River to assist Sister Catherina (Sister Madeline Murphy) in running the parish's very large Kindergarten. Sister Bertrand loved children and she wanted to develop her teaching skills. While in Powell River, Sister Bertrand studied education and obtained her teaching licence.

Sister Bertrand wrote "I enjoy working with little children and they seem to respond very well. We're happy together…While I am able, I shall always be ready to help out to the extent of my ability." She left Powell River in 1946 and later served with the Sisters of Charity of the Immaculate Conception teaching, working in an orphanage and ministering in parishes and serving the poor elsewhere. Falling ill with acute arthritis, Sister Bertrand retired from teaching but continued her ministry to the poor by knitting to raise funds for poor children. Although she knew that she was dying, she had no fear of death. She passed away at the Sisters of Charity Residence Home in Saint John New Brunswick in 1999.

Sister Mary Bertrand SCIC in Saint Joseph's Kindergarten. (1959, CoA)

In 1935, parishioner Walter Cavanaugh approached Father Corley and Father Hobson with an idea of setting up a mutual finance club in Powell River to help people finance the construction of their own homes. Father Hobson was receptive to the idea and in 1936, he organized a study group to look into the question as part of the parish's Holy Name Society, which ran an adult catechesis program. The first President of the Holy Name Society in Saint Joseph's parish was Carl Gaudet.

In the following years, Father Hobson began to preach on social themes related to financial assistance to those in need, following the social encyclicals of Pope Leo XIII. His activities drew so much interest that the study group attracted many parishioners and non-Catholics alike and the group began to meet in the parish hall. All of this activity led to the chartering of a Credit Union in 1939, which became the first Credit Union in British Columbia and from Powell River the idea spread to other communities in the province. Fr. Hobson himself left the parish in 1940 to join the Canadian air force for service in World War Two. He returned after the war to become pastor again in 1946.

The Society of the Holy Name is a confraternity for lay adult Catholics in care of the Dominican religious order. Society activities are centered on reverence for God and doing works of mercy in the parish surrounding community.

Saint Joseph's Parish. (1932, CoA)

During the 1940s and 1950s, Catholic communities were growing in outlying areas and for this reason additional community churches were built in Westview and Wildwood. At the time, few people had vehicles and it was a long walk from Wildwood or Westview to attend church services in Townsite.

Father Bourrie built Our Lady of the Angels Church on Joyce Avenue in Westview in 1940. The church was built by skilled and willing volunteers from the parish. After the construction of a second church in the parish, the Archbishop assigned an Assistant Pastor to the parish to help serve the community.

Our Lady of the Angels Catholic Church, Westview, Powell River. (CoA)

This church was later sold in the early 1960s to the Salvation Army and the building was later demolished. It was located on Joyce Avenue opposite First Credit Union.

In 1957 Father Joseph McInerney built Saint Gerard's Church in Wildwood. There was a strong desire within the parish to create local community churches in Wildwood and Cranberry that would allow people to attend mass in their own community without having to walk a far distance. Before the construction of Saint Gerard's parishioners walked down to Saint Joseph's from Wildwood crossing the bridge to attend mass on Sunday mornings. In the mid 1950s, there were approximately four hundred Catholics living in Wildwood, mainly recent Italian and Dutch immigrants. Fr. McInerny organized volunteer labour to construct the church which was large enough to hold 200 people. In 1957 Archbishop Duke came to the parish and blessed it as Saint Gerard's. After the Church's construction, members of the Italian community also used the basement as a meeting place for the Italian Club.

The Italian community initially concentrated in the area of Townsite near Saint Joseph's Church and then many Italians moved to Wildwood and Cranberry where they were free to plant large gardens and were free from the Townsite's rental houses owned by the Powell River Company. In fact, in the 1930s when many Italian workers lost their jobs at the hands of prejudiced discriminatory mill manager Joe Falconer. Local pastor Fr. Norbert Corley *O.Praem* advocated fiercely on their behalf.

Saint Gerard Majella—San Gerardo Maiella in Italian— was a beloved priest from Campania in southern Italy in the 1700s. He is the patron saint of expecting mothers, childbirth, children and the falsely accused. He is the universal patron for mothers and children and this devotion is especially popular in Italy.

Saint Gerard's Catholic Church, Wildwood, Powell River. (1958, CoA)

Saint Joseph's parish was fruitful for religious and priestly vocations, producing some very courageous and skilled ministers for the Church. Victor Gallo was an Italian immigrant born in Galleriano, Friuli. He grew up in Powell River and was ordained in 1947 and said his first Mass in St. Joseph's Church on June 2 that year. Fr. Gallo was known as a fun and holy man who set aside his summers to teach the faith to the youth.

In 1949, Aline Roulston, who had been working as a schoolteacher at Henderson Elementary School decided to join the Sisters of Charity of the Immaculate Conception.

John Swinkles, a Dutch immigrant to Canada, lived in Powell River for three years as a working seminarian, before being ordained as a priest at the Cathedral in 1954. He returned to Saint Joseph's on April 4, 1954 to say his inaugural mass in the community.

Then in 1956, Fay Trombley who was from Powell River also entered the Sisters of Charity of the Immaculate Conception.

All of these young vocations served the Church with a passion for the missions of the Church in more remote areas. In 1951, Father Gallo visited his hometown and he set off by boat on mission to visit remote communities further up the coast that were infrequently served by priests, saying masses at Squirrel Cove, Church House, Whaletown, Read Island, Redonda Bay and at work camps on Stuart Island, Minstrel Island and Gilford Island. An elderly woman living in Redonda Bay wrote to the Archbishop thanking him for sending Fr. Gallo, saying that she had not seen a Catholic priest in four years and that many other Catholics in the area had lapsed in their faith without access to the sacraments .

Like Fr. Gallo, Sr. Aline Roulston, also known as Sr. Robert Marie, enjoyed visiting and ministering to remote communities in rural Alberta, while she was teacher and guidance counsellor in Edmonton.

After a career as a schoolteacher, Sister Faye Trombley become the pastoral leader among Inuvialuit indigenous people in Tuktoyaktuk, a remote community in the Northwest Territories at Our Lady of Grace mission.

Father Victor Gallo's first mass, held in Saint Joseph's. He later became pastor in the 1970s and was very well suited to ministering to the needs of the faithful in this area, where the Catholic communities were small, poor and dispersed . He was very frugal and was dedicated to making long and dangerous trips in order to serve remote areas with the parish mission boat. He died in 2003 and is buried in Powell River.
(1950s, CoA)

Michael and Anne Savage

Anne (pronounced Annie) Savage was born in 1909 to the Donnelly family in Scotland and was betrothed to Michael Patrick Savage (b.1903) who emigrated to Canada to find work. In 1933, she left Scotland and joined Michael in Powell River where he had found work at the mill. They were married the following year and settled in the village of Westview. The couple had four children: Cecilia, Brian, Rose Ann and Bridget.

Anne and Michael lovingly filled their home with the four F's— faith, family, friends and fun. Michael Savage always carried his rosary in his pocket and he would pray two rosaries each day, one while going to work and one on the way home. They would also pray the rosary together as a family. Whenever Michael received his pay cheque, he always ensured to set aside his contribution in the church stipend envelope before spending anything.

Anne's taught her children the importance of loving their neighbours. She would regularly prepare baked goods for needy families or for important causes. In 1956/57 Anne was instrumental in supporting Hungarian refugees in Powell River, where she found them housing in Riverside and led clothing drives for their benefit.

Anne was a charter member of the Catholic Women's League and served the parish as a soloist at many weddings. Prayer and sacrifice were two virtues embodied by Anne and Michael. Michael passed away at the age of 63 in 1966. Anne remained an active member of the parish with an unwavering trust in God until her death at the age of 91 in 1998.

The Savage family (late 1950s, courtesy of Rose Anne Sole).
Anne Savage, Bridget and Michael (Front L to R) Kitty, Rose Anne, Brian and Cecilia (Back)

Italian immigrants first came to Powell River in 1910 to build the dam and town. Many of these men were single migrant labourers who didn't stay long in town but some settled and raised there families here. The second child born in the new town was Josie Mitchell from the Micheluzzi family born in 1911 and the first Catholic marriage recorded in town in 1913 was to an Italian couple. Over the next generation, one third of all baptisms registered in St Joseph's parish were for the children of Italian couples.

For this reason, from the 1950s, the parish offered an annual mission with Italian priests from as far away as New York. Initially at these missions, priests spent two weeks visiting every Italian household in the community, hearing confessions in Italian and preaching homilies in Italian—one week in Saint Joseph's and one week in the Church of the Angels. Many of the elderly Italians struggled to say confession in the English language and this pastoral care offered by the missions was a lifeline for them. These missions were an annual fixture in Powell River until the 1980s and were instrumental in keeping the Catholic faith alive in a difficult life with poverty, and culture shock adapting to a new homeland. In the 1980s, without the missions, the Italian speaking faithful were left cut off from the pastoral support they needed. In the 1990s, Fr. Hamilton revived this pastoral service and the parish again hosted Italian speaking priests annually offering mass and confessions in Italian.

(L) Italian Missionary Fr. Del Bo, (C) Fr. Joseph McInerney, (R) Fr. Eisenring
(L to R Altar Boys) Dante Galliazzo, Luke Bombardir

Italian members of the parish gather for the Italian mission in St Joseph's Church. (1955, Picture taken by Frank Dixon, CoA)

The character of Powell River changed dramatically in the 1950s with the opening of regular passenger ferry service from Saltery Bay to the Lower Sunshine Coast and Vancouver in 1954. The Black Ball Ltd Ferry company that operated the route was purchased by the Provincial Government in 1961, establishing BC Ferries. The ferries ended the era of steamship travel on the coast. It also caused the rapid growth of communities south of Powell River, most notably Westview, which would soon develop into the new heart of the parish.

Saint Joseph's Church was decorated with a very beautiful scene of the crucifixion with life-size statues of Mary, Saint John and Mary Magdalene under the cross, visually depicting the scene from the Gospel of John Chapter 19. This scene was at the focal point of the church, above the high altar that was attached to the back wall of Saint Joseph's Church.

Saint Joseph's Catholic Church during the visit of Canadian Prime Minister Saint Laurent in 1952. (1952, Picture taken by Frank Dixon, CoA)

During the mid twentieth century, oblate missionaries continued to serve the Tla'Amin Nation at Sacred Heart Church, the Klahoose Nation at Saint Peter's Church on Cortes Island and the Homalco Nation at Sacred Heart Church in Church House. The missionary priest would try to spend as much time as possible in each community, interacting with the families on each visit. Typical visits by the priests included daily masses, rosaries, benedictions, hearing confessions, and baptizing children.

Because of the distance, the priest did not visit each community on a weekly basis. The priest would travel to the Sliammon Reserve by ferry and bus from the Lower Sunshine Coast once a month and then every second week and would stay there for several days at a time. He would lead benediction, evening prayers and would say mass. He would also visit the families while there. At the time, there was an Altar Society which took up the role of fundraising and maintaining the church building.

During this time, lay leaders continued the old Tla'amin tradition of leading community worship, especially when there was no priest in town. Sandy Timothy, who owned a Roman Missal, led prayers at funerals in the absence of a priest. Either Sandy Timothy or his brother Chief Tom Timothy would lead the congregation for worship on the weeks when no priest was present to say mass. Sammy Adams served as the bellman and would ring the church bell before mass. Ambrose Wilson, originally from Church House, decorated the church at Christmas time and whenever the bishop visited, paying for it with his own personal money.

(Sechelt District, 1957. BCA #A00826..29.14)

The congregation after mass, Sacred Heart Church, Sliammon.
Father Vernon Joseph Campbell OMI back row. (c. 1937, CoA)

The oblate missionary priest would visit Squirrel Cove by boat from Vancouver once a month and Church House (ʔop̓) by boat from Vancouver for one week long visits at a time less often. At Saint Peter's Church on Cortes Island the priest would say mass and lead prayers for the small community at toq̓. The priest would visit Sacred Heart Church at Church House for about one week at a time on major feast days. While there, he would lead missions, offer the sacraments, lead prayers and benediction.

It was common that some non-native Catholics who lived or worked on nearby islands would seek out the priest during his visit and would join the First Nations in worship. Since many of these individuals and families rarely had the opportunity to attend a functioning church, the priest would hear many confessions and baptize children who were presented to him during his stay. Some of the children were baptized at much older ages than what was common in cities as a result.

(Sechelt District, 1957. BCA #A00826..29.14)

Sacred Heart Church at the right, Church House.
(mid 20th century, CoA)

The Church of the Assumption

Father John Collins became pastor in Saint Joseph's parish in 1958, sent by Archbishop Duke with the assignment to build a new church and school for the parish. The new pastor had foresight to realize that with the arrival of a ferry connection to the Sunshine Coast, the town was growing considerably to the South towards Westview and the ferry terminal. Fr. Collins was amazed by the large number of Catholic children in each of the neighbourhoods and the crowded conditions in the small Our Lady of the Angels Church in Westview and believed that the parish was in desperate need of a larger church and a parish school in Westview.

With the support of parish organizations like the CWL, Fr. Collins began fundraising, and planning the construction of a new Church and parish school. The parish then sold Our Lady of the Angles Church to the Salvation Army and purchased a vacant lot in Westview, which would become the Church of the Assumption and Assumption School. The initial plans also included a convent and rectory in a massive Church and School complex. The project was realized by Doyle Bros. Construction of Vancouver.

Father Collins then closed Saint Joseph's Kindergarten and sent the Sisters of Charity of the Immaculate Conception away from the parish because they were unable to provide teachers for an entire Catholic school. After their departure, parishioners and non-parishioners who had gone to the Kindergarten at Saint Joseph's continued to remember the sisters and St. Joseph's Kindergarten with warm affection.

The original design of a Assumption Church complex as presented to the parish by Father Collins that was intended to include the school, the rectory, and a convent. (1959, CoA)

Assumption Church and Assumption School opened in 1961. The Church was completed one year before Pope John XXIII convened the Second Vatican Council. For this reason, the Church was initially built following traditional Catholic architectural plans with a high altar attached to the back wall. The first masses in the Church likewise were said in the traditional Latin form, as had always been the case in the parish up until the 1960s.

In the following few years, the liturgical changes that came out of the Second Vatican Council were implemented in the parish by Father Collins in the mid 1960s. The first noticeable change was having the local vernacular language, English, replace Latin as the principal language of worship. As well, the high altar was removed and replaced by a free standing altar in the middle of the sanctuary.

Fr. Collins celebrates the Savage wedding in the new Church of the Assumption. (1961, CoA)

Church of the Assumption, Westview Powell River. (2001, CoA)

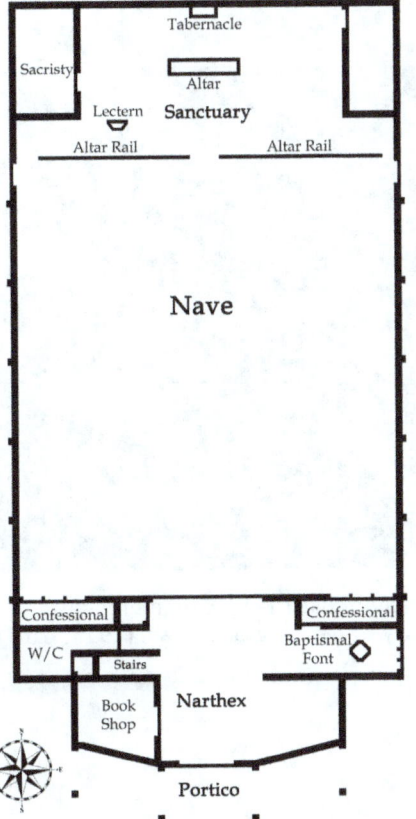

Floor plan of the Church of the Assumption after being adapted to liturgical changes of the mid 1960s. (Reconstruction)

The period immediately following the Second Vatican council was a period of considerable change for Saint Joseph's parish. There was an increase in the number of the faithful frequenting the sacraments during the period. The parish was young, with over half of the members under the age of 21 and growing with 110 baptisms and 40 marriages in 1967 alone. Father O'Grady was appointed pastor in 1967 and he was known as a leader for the liturgical reform in the Archdiocese. He established an elected parish committee, that was the precursor to the Parish Council, which successive pastors composed of nominated members from different parish groups. In 1969, a liturgical committee was set up to address practical changes about organizing Sunday worship. It was intended to help win over many parishioners who were uncomfortable with the liturgical changes. The main goal of the liturgical renewals was to encourage lay participation in the mass, especially in singing hymns.

The directives in *Inter Oecumenici* that followed the Second Vatican Council encouraged the installation of freestanding altars in Catholic Churches rather than high altars and other modification to the sanctuary. The permanent modifications of the sanctuary in the Church of the Assumption would take several decades to realize. During the 1970s, Father Gallo replaced the temporary altar with a new large marble free standing altar.

(Inter Oecumenici, 2, 91, 95.; Parish Reports 1968, 1970)

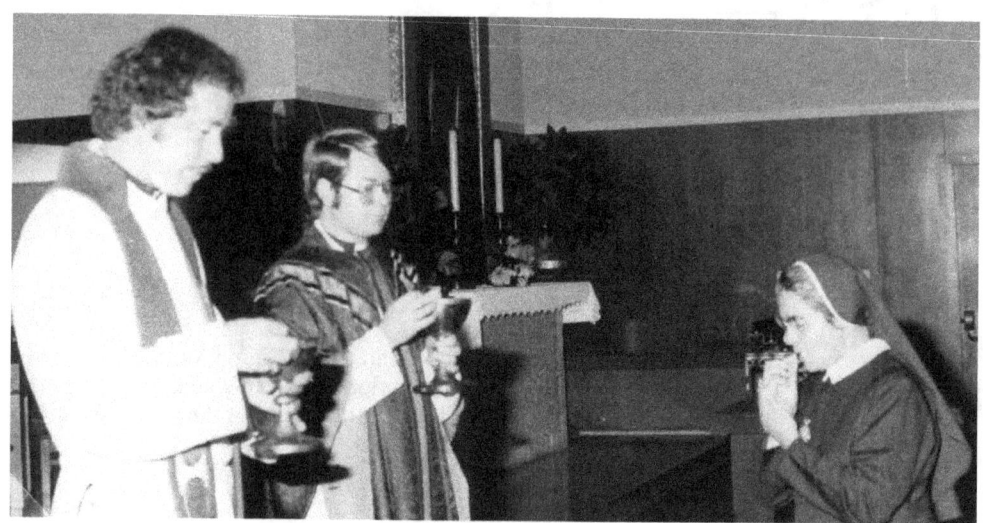

Father Glenn Dion and Father John Eason administer Holy Communion to Sister Concetta for her Twenty Fifth Anniversary of her religious vows. (1978, CoA)

The first major challenge that faced Assumption School was finding teachers to staff the school. In 1961, Father Collins was urged by Joseph Formosa parishioner from Malta to appeal to Bishop Galea of Malta and ask if his diocese in Malta could provide the parish with nuns to teach at the school. Assumption School opened in September of 196.1 Fr. Collins hired temporary lay teachers to teach until the Sisters arrived in Powell River. Soon after, six sisters from the Missionaries of Jesus of Nazareth were chosen to respond to the call and they flew from Malta to Powell River. When they arrived in Vancouver, they spent one week visiting schools and teachers in the city. They arrived in Powell River on Thanksgiving day and started teaching as the regular classroom teachers at the brand new Assumption Catholic School on the following day. They faithfully taught the BC curriculum from day one.

Initially, the school run from grades one through seven and there were six sisters teaching and one lay teacher. Sister Petronilla served as the school's first principal and she also taught the grade seven class. Later in the 1960s, layman Frank Rigby joined the school and assumed the role as its principal. Over the years, additional sisters came to Powell River from Malta to the expanding school to add to the teaching staff and also replace several sisters who returned to Malta.

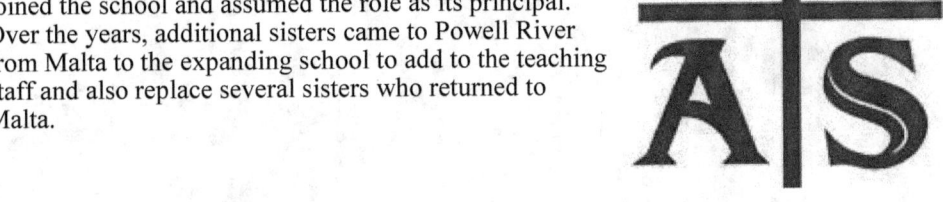

Principal Frank Rigby in Grade 7 class at Assumption School. (1969, CoA)

The Missionary Sisters of Jesus of Nazareth also provided for the spiritual needs of the parish, by giving religious instruction to those non attending Assumption School, visiting the sick and elders and leading retreats at Squirrel Cove and Church House. They established the Mater Ecclesiae convent in Westview.

Arrival of the Missionary Sisters of Jesus of Nazareth in Canada. (1961, CoA)

Sister Claire Sappiano teaching Kindergarten at Assumption School. (1980s, CoA)

In 1967, Archbishop Johnson urged Saint Joseph's parish to expand its ministry to surrounding areas. In 1969, the Archbishop of Vancouver assigned a third priest, Fr. Terry Conway OMI, to Saint Joseph's parish along with the request to provide for the spiritual needs of the territories formerly served by the oblate missionaries. This allowed Saint Joseph's Pastor O'Grady to provide regular mass at Sacred Heart Church on the Sliammon Reserve and mass every second Sunday in Vananda on Texada Island. For the first time in the history of the Sacred Heart Church, it was possible to offer reliable weekly masses to the Tla'amin Nation.

The Star of the Sea III which had been serving Ocean Falls, near Bella Coola was given to the parish in Powell River by Archbishop Johnson in 1967 so that the parish could meet his request to serve the outlying areas only accessible by water. The boat was named *stella maris*, the star of the sea, after the Virgin Mary. It was like a chapel and had an altar built onto the back of the cabin. The priests would travel by the Star of the Sea to Vananda on the island of Texada, saying mass at the United Church there. The priest would also travel to Squirrel Cove and Church House by the Star of the Sea to celebrate mass at major festivities.

Ambrose Wilson's fishing boat towing the Star of the Sea, the parish mission boat on a trip to Church House for a summer camp . The boat had mechanical problems and was towed into port. (1971, CoA)

Fr. O'Grady asked school principal Frank Rigby to run the mission boat as its captain and he regularly transported each of the three priests to Texada, Squirrel Cove and Church House from the boat's moorage in Westview Harbour. Voyages up the coast to Squirrel Cove and Church House were infrequent due to safety concerns in poor winter weather and it took many hours for the boat to reach the destinations. However, they were always well received and masses in those communities were well attended.

In the summers during the late 1960s and 1970s, the Missionary Sisters of Jesus of Nazareth took groups parish youth up to Church House to run a summer school and teach Catechism to the children there. At that time, the Missionary Sisters of Christ the King, a religious order founded in Montreal in 1930 by Sister Frédérica Giroux, known locally as the Snow Nuns, also taught at the local school in Church House.

Assumption Catholic School also occasionally used the Star of the Sea for school camps on Cortes Island. The Star of the Sea stayed with the parish until 1978, when it was sent to serve Camp Latona, on Gambier Island. After that, priests travelled by Ferry to Texada and to go to Squirrel Cove and Church House by the Sliammon Band boat.

Archbishop Carney, Father Victor Gallo and Missionary Sisters of Christ the King (MCR) after arriving at Church House on the Star of the Sea. (c. 1976, CoA)

Fr Gallo blesses cedar boughs for Palm Sunday festivities at Sacred Heart Church in Church House. The cedar branches have traditional spiritual significance and were used in place of palms and to decorate the crucifix inside of the church. (1971, CoA)

Sisters of Jesus of Nazareth on a visit to Squirrel Cove, Cortes Island at a time when the Saint Peter's Church was being restored. (1970s, CoA)

Missionary Sisters of Jesus of Nazareth (M.S.J.N.)

Order's Motto: "Jesus of Nazareth Who I have seen and loved."

The Congregation of the Missionary Sisters of Jesus of Nazareth was founded in Malta by Miss Guzeppina Curmi with the charismas of Simplicity, Humility and Charity. The order was formally erected by the Archbishop of Malta in 1934.

The mission in Powell River was one of the order's main missions outside of its home of Malta. Apart from teaching at Assumption School, the Sisters taught C.C.D. to the many children who attended public school. They also made home visits in the parish on weekends and holidays, visited the sick in the hospital, the elderly in the Extended Care Unit and in their homes. The sisters also served as Eucharistic ministers, supported the Faith and Light program, and worked with the First Nations.

(Back Row Left to Right) Sister Michelina and Sister Rose
(Front Row Left to Right) Sister Agostina, Petronilla and Claire
((1990s, CoA)

Sister Agostina Scicluna , M.S.J.N.

Sister Agostina Scicluna was born in 1924 in the town of Żebbuġ, Malta and grew up reading pamphlets about missions in India and Africa. She always used to say, "When I grow up I will become a nurse, go to the convent to look after the sick people." In 1951, at the age of twenty-seven, she joined the Missionary Sisters of Jesus of Nazareth where she took care of orphaned and abandoned children at their convent in Malta. To her surprise in 1961, the Mother General asked her to go to teach at the Assumption Catholic School in Powell River, BC. She accepted this as God's Will for her and left Malta in October 1961 along with five other sisters. Once in Powell River, she loved teaching the children and when she was not in school she would go and visit the sick or someone whom she thought would like a visit. She taught for thirty four years at Assumption School, retiring in 1995 at the age of seventy-one. After retiring, she continued to help the school, teach Catechism and make pastoral visits to the elderly.

At the end of her life, she never complained, even when she was in great pain. She confounded her doctor when he told her that she had terminal cancer by calmly responding, "It's ok. It's God's will." On Sister Agostina's last day, her doctor asked her how she was feeling and quickly she raised her hand indicating that she was going to meet Our Lord. Father Agius then celebrated mass for her with her fellow sisters and fellow teacher Bridget Bigold. She passed away in 2009 in Powell River at the age of 84.

Sister Agostina at Haywire Bay (1996, CoA)

Lay community members have assumed different roles at Sacred Heart Church since regular mass and a parish structure were introduced in the 1970s. Ida August used to walk into Powell River to get fresh flowers for mass and then would go to the church with a clock and ring the church bell every fifteen minutes on Sunday morning before mass. Lily Francis and her daughter Elsie Paul both served the community in the linen care ministry, carefully washing and pressing the linen cloths that are used in the sacred liturgy. In more recent years, Betty Wilson, Joe Wilson, Debbie Wilson and Mary Harry have taken on the role of caring for Sacred Heart Church, especially making it beautiful for the Christmas celebration.

In the 1970s, Dr. Elsie Paul arranged with Sister Petronilla for the Sisters to provide Catechism for Tla'amin children in Sliammon, since families whose children attended public schools found it difficult to drive them to Catechism program at Assumption Church in Westview. They then organized a weekly CCD program every Thursday in Sacred Heart Church that was very well attended.

(*A Dream that Came True*. P.11)

Archbishop James Carney, Father Victor Gallo, Fr Larkin, Fr Eason and Missionary Sisters of Jesus of Nazareth with the First Communion class at Sacred Heart Church, Sliammon. (c. 1976, CoA)

Since the 19th century, it has been customary for the Bishops and Archbishops of the diocese to visit Catholics annually, especially to administer the sacrament of confirmation and often to be present for first holy communions as well.

During the late 1970s and early 1980s, Saint Joseph's parish reduced the number of churches it served and reduced the number of priests that were part of the parish.

After Fr. Gallo was reassigned in 1979, the parish gave up the Star of the Sea parish boat. This was done because unlike Fr. Gallo who was a skilled boater, the subsequent priests assigned to the parish from the city were uncomfortable operating a boat and preferred to travel either by ferry or by the Sliammon band boat. Later, in 1979 following the decision by the inhabitants of Church House to relocate elsewhere, the parish stopped providing mass at Church House. A few years later, in the early 1980s, the Archbishop decided to reduce the parish to only two priests and Father Dickinson decided to stop offering mass at Saint Peter's Church on Cortes Island.

The absence of an active church was hard on the faithful left behind in toq̓. Klahoose elder Lily Hill continued to pray on her own until 2015 when Tla'amin elder Betty Wilson arranged for Archbishop J. Michael Miller CSB to visit her on Cortes Island. She was in disbelief that the Archbishop would make the trip all the way from Vancouver to see her. She said this visit was the most special moment in her life and that she could now die in peace. Lily Hill passed away in 2016.

Sacred Heart Church, Church House after its closure. It has since collapsed. (1980s, CoA)

In 1978, parishioners from the Italian community spearheaded an initiative to create a publicly owned mausoleum at the Cranberry cemetery. The Powell River Regional District approved the project, introducing the traditional Italian custom of a mausoleum in Powell River. The mausoleum finally opened on October 20, 1982 with Fr. Dickenson and Fr. Dion, head of the Powell River ministerial association blessing the burial place.

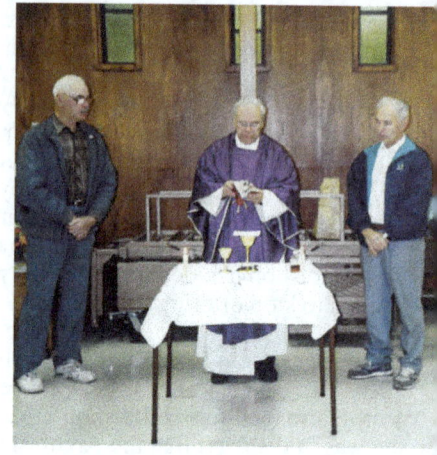

Fr. Gallo says mass in the Mausoleum i with Tony Bombadir and Elio Cossarin (1998, Courtesy of Elio Cossarin)

In 1931, three young Italian workers Primo Gobbo (26), Giuseppe Morello (29) and Giovanni Peloso (33) fell one hundred feet to their deaths down a disused chimney after their scaffold collapsed at the mill. One worker, family man Luigi Gallegari, remarkably survived the accident, though he was deeply scarred by it. The tragedy shocked Powell River as a whole and traumatized Italian parishioners in particular.

In 1997, parishioners arranged for plaques to be installed over the tombs of the three deceased workers who had been buried in unmarked graves in 1931, since they had no family. Father Victor Gallo celebrated mass in their honor at the mausoleum. Father Gallo was a boy at the time of the accident and he recalled that his own father had nearly been assigned to be part of that fateful chimney crew that day in 1931.

Tombs of the fallen workers Primo Gobbo, Giuseppe Morello and Giovanni Peloso with the plaques. (1997, Courtesty of Elio Cossarin).

When Father Collins conceived of the new Assumption Church and Assumption School in the late 1950s, the initial plan included a parish hall and rectory. These, however, were not built for financial reasons and, as a result, the existing rectory and Our Lady of Good Counsel Hall both active parts of the parish into the 1980s.

Early in the 1980s, the new pastor, Father Dickinson, made the decision to build a new rectory above Assumption School and the Church of the Assumption. He then closed Saint Joseph's Church in Townsite and sold the church building, the rectory and hall. The new rectory building eventually was to contain a chapel upstairs, used by the priests for private worship.

Following the closure of Saint Joseph's Church, Saint Joseph's Parish became unofficially known as the Church of the Assumption. This usage stuck and eventually the parish changed its name to the Church of the Assumption.

The new Rectory next to Assumption School and the Church of the Assumption.
(1983, CoA)

In 1989, a new bell tower was added to Saint Gerard's Church in Wildwood. The church also became the new home to a very beautiful crucifix that had formerly been in Saint Joseph's Church, until it was closed in 1983.

Saint Gerard's Catholic Church with its new bell tower, Wildwood , Powell River (1989, CoA)

Saint Gerard's Catholic Church, Wildwood , Powell River
Living Rosary in Saint Gerard's Church. (2011, CoA)

A notable change at Assumption School was the gradual replacement of the Missionary Sisters of Jesus of Nazareth with lay teachers. The last religious teacher to retire was sister Claire Sapiano in 2008, after forty years of teaching at the school. In 2012, Sister Claire and Sister Rose decided to return to Malta to spend out their retirement there in the mother house of the Missionary Sisters of Jesus of Nazareth.

The Mater Ecclesiae convent in Westview was sold when they left. It became the first time since the 1930s that the parish in Powell River ceased to be the home of religious sisters. Their departure has changed the parish, which has struggled to fill the large hole left by their absence, particularly their skill in offering catechetical support for the young in public school and their commitment to visiting the sick, and elderly, especially in the Tla'amin nation. Since the departure of the Sisters from Powell River, the parish has struggled to replicate the solid Christian witness in the wider community and many good pastoral works previously provided by the sisters.

Mater Ecclesiae Convent, Westview, Powell River. (CoA)

The Catholic Women's League

Since being founded in 1935, the Catholic Women's League has remained the Catholic organization for women in Assumption Parish. The Catholic's Women's League has continued to be very involved over the years in the parish activities. They have regularly led campaigns to raise funds for the needs of the local church.

In the 1960s alone, the CWL raised funds to restore churches, support a parish mission in Peru, purchase Catechism resources, create a scholarship funds, support the Hospital Auxiliary and help finance the foundation of Olive Devaud Seniors Home. The CWL ran activities on Texada starting in the 1960s, where they organized a children's choir and a Christmas party.

(Sitting L to R) Andy Culos, Fr. Collins (Standing) Theresa Venables, Josie Mitchell, Mary Schreurs, Julie Moretto, Lorraine Behan, Mona Knight, Ruth Culos

Catholic Women's League at a farewell party for Father John Collins in 1967.
(Picture taken by Frank Dixon, KOC Council 5417 Archives)

The Catholic Women's League

More recent CWL activities include providing annual Christmas hampers to needy families, assisting meals on wheels , supporting Pro-Life initiatives, promoting an anti-pornography campaign, fundraising for parish youth to attend World Youth Days and raising funds for refugees sponsored by the parish.

The parish hosted twenty-six Vietnamese refugees in 1980 and supported an entire Syrian family in 2016. The CWL continues to address problematic legislative issues and takes action on resolutions as needed with letters, petitions, and visits to council meetings, MLAs and MPs.

In addition to all these special initiatives, the CWL has constantly promoted a joyous atmosphere in the parish through the parish bazaar and its support of regular festivities throughout the year.

(Sitting L to R) Mary Ann Johnson, Fr. Dickinson, (Standing) Agata Lucato, Betty Hoy, Bridget Bigold, Bernadette Martinuk, Bernice Anstat

Catholic Women's League host a 70th birthday party for Father Dickinson.
(Picture by Frank Dixon, 1988, CoA)

Knights of Columbus Council 5417—Powell River

A group of former Knights of Columbus in St. Joseph's Parish were hoping to set up a Council in Powell River in late 1940s but plans were delayed due to the community's isolation. Their hopes were finally realized when Father John Collins became pastor in 1958 and road and ferry links had been established to both Vancouver and Vancouver Island. The Council was formed on April 20, 1963. The first Chaplain was Father John Collins and the first Grand Knight was Andy Culos.

The new Knights council purchased and donated an ambulance to Powell River. Grand Knight Kip Sluggett presents this gift to City Reeve Dave Pike in 1967. (above) (Picture by Frank Dixon, KOC Council 5417 Archives)

Knights of Columbus Council 5417—Powell River

Original Formation Knights of Columbus, June 15, 1963 (above).

Back Row (L-R) Leslie Adams, Dante Galliazzo, Felix Massullo, Stewart Long, Mike O'Rielly, Ken Culos, Elio Cossarin, John Bogoslowski, Harry Carr, Gerry de Groot, Lionel Desilets

Seated on Stage (L-R) Jack Tromley, Charlie Bombardir, John Elder, Kevin O'Hara, Tom Behan, John Straathof, Bernie De Jong, John Zuccato, Kip Sluggett, Fred McLeod, Babe Mitchell

Standing on Floor (L-R) F.W. Dixon, Peter Egbert, Wilfred Buckley, Paul Madden, Paddy Behan, Danny Behan, Gerry Behan, Gindo Culos, Hilbert Long, Gene Strubey, Art Barrett, Hugh Meville

Seated on Floor (L-R) William Brown, Henry De Chaine, Phil Knight, Henry Culos, Murray Doyle, Andy Culos, Re. Fr. McDonnel, Adrian Schreurs, Hector Oxberry, Len Hocken, Peter Grabowski

Since 1963, the Knights of Columbus Council 5417 has been the fraternal Catholic organization for men in Assumption Parish.

The Knights of Columbus raise funds for the community, support parish initiatives and have social functions for the members. The knights purchased smoke detectors throughout the Olive Devaud home for seniors, offered scholarships for local students, and regularly supported the parish with manpower and fundraising. The council works closely with Assumption Parish, providing funds for various projects. Knights annual Charity Appeal ticket sales earn approximately $4000 for various charities. In 1991, the KOC purchased the old Powell River Golf Club house in Townsite to use as a hall.

A few interesting things to note are three brothers have served as Grand Knights, Patrick Tom and Dan Behan. A father and two sons have also been Grand Knights, Lionel, Rolland and Jerome Desilets. Don Bourcier has served as Grand Knight on 3 different occasions for a 2 year term each.

The knights provide a monthly pancake breakfast for the parish and graduation breakfast and Catholic School week. They host the annual parish golf tournament and Ladies Night Dinner and Dance in May and a games night in February. They run a 'Keep Christ in Christmas' campaign in November and December and keep a section of our highway clean as part of the 'Adopt a Highway' program.

Nick Amato, Cam Dubord, Roland Drouin, Ron Spreeuw, Don Bourcier (Grand Knight), Fraser Field, Raymond Pinel, Robert Bruke, Jim Landry (District Warden), Mariusz Wernerowski, Henry Ortynski, Fred Rhodes, Al Astles (District Deputy), Walter Temple, Bruno Canil, Lionel Desilets. (L to R).
(KOC Council 5417 Archives)

Faith and Light is an ecumenical group born of a desire to help people with an intellectual disability and their families find their place within the Church and society. Faith and Light Communities consist of groups of 15 to 40 persons (children, teenagers or adults with an intellectual disability, their family, friends) who meet together at least once per month for a gathering of friendship, sharing, prayer and celebration. Their mission in the community is to create bonds of friendship between all members and to reveal to each person his/her unique gift and beauty. Faith and Light, born at the heart of the Roman Catholic Church, is an ecumenical movement. It is founded on the conviction that persons with an intellectual disability have been chosen by God to confound the wise and the strong.

Faith and Light was inspired and follows the teaching of Jean Vanier and was brought to Powell River by Elio and Bernadette Cossarin in 1984 with support of the parish and the Missionary Sisters. Meetings follow a religious theme and include learning about the topic, songs, artistic projects on the theme and questions and answers. Above all its is a group of friendship and prayer.

(Front L to R) Albert Martin, Elio Cossarin, Vincent Heslin, Bernadette Cossarin, Joan Gatt, Monica Martin, Mary Behan (Back) Peter Cossarin, Louise Ikachuk, Vivian Kaban, Elaine Pighin, Theresa Bourassa, Mary Johnson, Rory Bell, Kay Johnson, Larry Evans, Mary Hicks

Faith and Light gathering at the Martin Residence at Pebble Beach, 1993. (1993, CoA)

PRO-LIFE and Birthright

The Powell River Pro Life organization had its origins in 1972 when Dr. Murphy and Father Gallo made a slide presentation to the parish about abortion, which had been partially legalized in Canada in 1969.

Abortions began to be administered in the Powell River hospital in 1969. In 1972, the Pro-Life group formed and it has always been an ecumenical organization attracting Christians from all denominations since.

The Pro-Life organization strived hard to elect Pro-Life candidates to the local hospital board. Eventually, this led to a victory in 1987 when the local hospital board decided to stop administering abortions at the Powell River General Hospital.

Powell River Birthright opened in 1977 to help women, men and families who were troubled by an unplanned pregnancy. Bernie Cossarin and Margaret Tyrne were the first volunteers and they provided emergency pregnancy support in homes. By 2003, there were 18 volunteers. The Knights of Columbus and Catholic Church were the organization's biggest supporters. Birthright operated an office in Powell River from 1977 until 2007.

(L to R) Lionel Desilets, Denise Jablonsky, Dr. Frank Murphy, Anne Desilets, Annette Massullo, Pat Clark, Phil Knight

Knight of Columbus present Pro Life and Birthright activists received a certificate of recognition for their efforts in 1981.
(Picture by Frank Dixon, KoC Council 5417 Archives)

In 1992, the Pro-Life group opened its own office in Powel River, that it maintained for twenty years. The office focused on providing information to youth about the realities of abortion and offering post–abortion support to those in need of help.

The group continues to be involved in Pro-Life walks and prayers outside of places where abortions are performed. The group leads the annual Walk for Life, which has involved hundreds of local walkers and spread awareness of the Pro Life cause since 1992. The Society has regular monthly meetings and is an ecumenical organization. Everyone is welcome and encouraged to attend.

(L to R) Fred MacLeod, Pat Clark, Crol Oyer, Marta Cecchi, Eva Dobozy, Kinga Dobozy, Marg MacLeod

Local Pro-Life members on the Saltery Bay Ferry participating in a Walk for Life across Canada (2000s, CoA).

Monument in memory of the unborn, located to the left of the main entrance of Assumption Church. Projected and spearheaded by Elio and Bernadette Cossarin.

Maranatha (Come Lord Jesus) Prayer Group

Maranatha Prayer Group is part of the Catholic Charismatic Renewal that spread through the Catholic Church following the Second Vatican Council. Many parishioners participated in ecumenical Charismatic prayer groups during the 1970s and 1980s.

Maranatha is a charismatic prayer group that meets once a week year round to praise God in prayer and song, to listen to the word of God, to share their journeys and pray for each other and the needs of the parish and the world. Members are active in our parish and over the years have put on yearly Life in the Spirit Seminars, led many programs open to the whole parish, brought in outstanding speakers, provided coffee and muffins once a month after the morning mass, plus helped out at many parish functions. When Archbishop Adam Exner became bishop of Vancouver he allowed the first Charismatic Conference in Vancouver in 1992. A large group of our parishioners attended the Conference in 1997 and were inspired to form their own prayer group. Theresa and Ray Pinel approached Father Hamilton in November for permission to run a "Life in the Spirit Seminar" in January 1998. He gave his blessing and after the Seminars in March 1998, which happened to be the year of the Holy Spirit, the Maranatha Prayer was formed. It has run continuously since then.

(L to R - Front)—Theresa and Ray Pinel.
(Back) — Charlene Bourcier, Pierina Canil, Peggy Lacourciere, Yvonne Morrissey, Landi Bledstone, Don Bourcier, Pat Clark, Roland Drouin.

Maranatha Prayer Group.(2009, CoA)

Assumption School has thrived despite being the only rural school among the many Catholic Independent Schools in the Archdiocese of Vancouver. The distinct character of the school is tailored to serving the needs of a vast and isolated parish community. The school itself has been one of the parish's main pastoral initiatives. Like St. Joseph's Kindergarten before it, Assumption School has been a successful outreach program to many non-Catholic families. As well, parishioners and the school children come together to worship as one Friday mornings at weekday mass.

Saint Joseph's Academy (1995, CoA)

Assumption School followed the lead of the local SD47 school district, expanded itself and established a Middle School, Saint Joseph's Academy in 1995, with financial aid from the Archdiocese of Vancouer's from Proejct Advance fund.

Statue of Our Lady of the Assumption relocated from the Mater Ecclesiae convent to the side entrance of Assumption School. (2016, CoA)

Assumption Catholic School holds an annual Christmas Concert for family and friends. The concert showcases the students from all grades singing Christmas carols, playing Christmas music and performing Christmas themed plays. The school is also active in Powell River extracurricular sporting activities.

Assumption School Christmas Concert (2013, CoA)

Assumption School Girls Volleyball Team, Powell River Champions . (2008, CoA)

Bridget Bigold

Bridget was born in 1952, the youngest child of the loving and devout parents Michael and Anne Savage. She was raised in Powell River, attended Saint Joseph's parish and Assumption Catholic School from when the school was first opened. Bridget married Dennis Bigold and went on to have three children Rachelle, Jacqueline and Brent.

Bridget was a remarkable woman who served the parish community and Assumption School where she taught Grade 6 for many years. She was a leader of Saint Gerard's Church in Wildwood, among others served on the PEC, PREP, Religious instruction, the Parish Council, the Catholic Women's League, and Birth Right.

If someone was sick she would cook a meal and take it to the family. If you needed any assistance be sure that she was there to help you. Each morning she would get up early to prepare breakfast for her husband, then would sit at the dinning room table by the window with the Bible and make her meditation and say some prayers.

At a young age Bridget had cancer and was away for a long time at the hospital but she never complained about pain or anything and she really was in pain but instead she tried to smile and joke with those who went to visit her. She remained a courageous and faithful leader of the parish until her death in 2015 at the age of 63

Bridget Bigold in Saint Joseph's Hall (2013, CoA)

During the 1980s, Father Dickinson made considerable physical changes to Assumption Church. He replaced a curtain that was hanging behind the altar with oak panelling. He also removed the two side altars and replaced them with wooden shelves for the statues of Our Lady and Saint Joseph.

During the 1990s, the next pastor, Father Hamilton, made further changes to Assumption Church. He beautified the sanctuary with marble work. He also installed a small marble altar for the tabernacle including marble additions to the pulpit, decorated with traditional Christian symbols. His intention was to harmonize the main altar of the Eucharistic Sacrifice with the altar of the Word.

Father Hamilton at reading from the new marble lectern. (2010, CoA)

The Greek letters IC XC represent Jesus Christ and the Greek letters NIKA spell the Greek word NIKA for 'victory,' remembering Christ's victory over death.

Church of the Assumption Choirs

The Senior Choir has sung at the morning mass at the Church of the Assumption. Once a month, the Senior Choir sings the hymns in Latin, whereas on the other Sundays the hymns are sung only in English.

Senior Choir. (2009, CoA)

The Junior Choir sings the hymns at the Sunday evening mass at Assumption church.

In 2007, Frances Schweitzer organized a new choir for those interested in singing traditional hymns at the 7pm mass. Over the next few years, the choir transitioned into a children's choir and the kids were keen to learn Latin hymns and picked up the *Missa Primitiva*. At the time, many of the children were in their primary grades and the organist who was barely twelve years old. As the choir gained confidence in chant, they embarked on polyphony.

As well as singing at mass and the festival, the children are often asked to sing at funerals and understanding this to be a corporal work of mercy, they are keen to do so as often as they are able. There is the hope that these children will continue in this important ministry as they graduate and move into adulthood.

Junior Choir performing Ave Maris Stella at the Festival of the Performing Arts.
(2016, CoA)

In 2013, the parish's junior choir decided to share some liturgical music with the community at the Festival of the Performing Arts. The kids were very keen to perform and chose to enter singing very challenging a capella songs. They have impressed both the adjudicator and the audience. They have performed:

The Wisdom of God" by Heath Morber   O Sanctissima by Kevin Allen.
Lord, You Have Searched Me, by Handel Ecce Panis Angelorum (anoymous)
O Salutaris, by Muller   Panis Angelicus, by Kevin Allen
Paratur, Kevin Allen   O Sacrum Convivium, Allen
Ave Maris Stella by Saint Saens

O sanctissima, o piissima, *dulcis Virgo Maria!* *Mater amata, intemerata,* *ora, ora pro nobis.*	O most holy, o most loving, sweet Virgin Mary! Beloved Mother, undefiled, pray, pray for us.
Tu solatium et refugium, *Virgo Mater Maria.* *Quidquid optamus, per te speramus;* *ora, ora pro nobis.*	You are solace and refuge, Virgin, Mother Mary. Whatever we wish, we hope it through you; pray, pray for us.
Ecce debiles, perquam flebiles; *salva nos, o Maria!* *Tolle languores, sana dolores;* *ora, ora pro nobis.*	Look, we are weak and deeply deplorable; save us, o Mary! Take away our lassitude, heal our pains; pray, pray for us.
Virgo, respice, Mater, aspice; *audi nos, o Maria!* *Tu medicinam portas divinam;* *ora, ora pro nobis.*	Virgin, look at us, Mother, care for us; hear us, o Mary! You bring divine medicine; pray, pray for us.

In 2008, the parish consecrated Saint Joseph's Hall. It is a large two-storey building next to the Church of the Assumption; its facilities are of use to the parish, parish groups, the school and the parish soup kitchen.

The completion of Saint Joseph's Hall moved the parish one step closer to realizing Father Collins' original vision of the Church of the Assumption. It also gave the parish once again access to its own hall, over twenty years after the sale of its former hall, the Our Lady of Good Counsel Hall in Townsite.

Saint Joseph's Hall next to the Church of the Assumption on the left (above) and from the street (below). (2008, CoA)

Saint Joseph's Hall gathering for the Sacrament of Confirmation in 2011. (2011, CoA)

Floor mosaic of Saint Joseph and the child Jesus at the entryway to Saint Joseph's Hall. (2011, CoA)

In 2014, Father Teeporten gave permission to the youth group to renovate St. Gerard's basement into a cozy and vibrant area to be used by parish youth and a meeting place.

The refurbished basement is now used as a meeting place for parishioners who attend mass at Saint Gerard's, as well as youth rosaries and teas. (2014,CoA)

The Assumption Community Soup Kitchen

During Lent in 2015, Christine Behan, inspired by the call to 'feed the hungry,' realized that there was a need for a soup kitchen for the needy on Fridays in Powell River. She opened Assumption Soup Kitchen in April 2015.

The soup kitchen now serves lunch every Friday in Saint Joseph's Hall and everyone is welcome. It is operated by of volunteers and has received strong backing from the CWL and several community businesses.

The Assumption Community Soup Kitchen serves up healthy, home-cooked meals. It strives to make everyone feel welcome and important. Volunteers put a lot of love into their cooking and feel that everyone who comes is treated like family. Many seniors who come for the social time, as well as young families and even business people at times come.

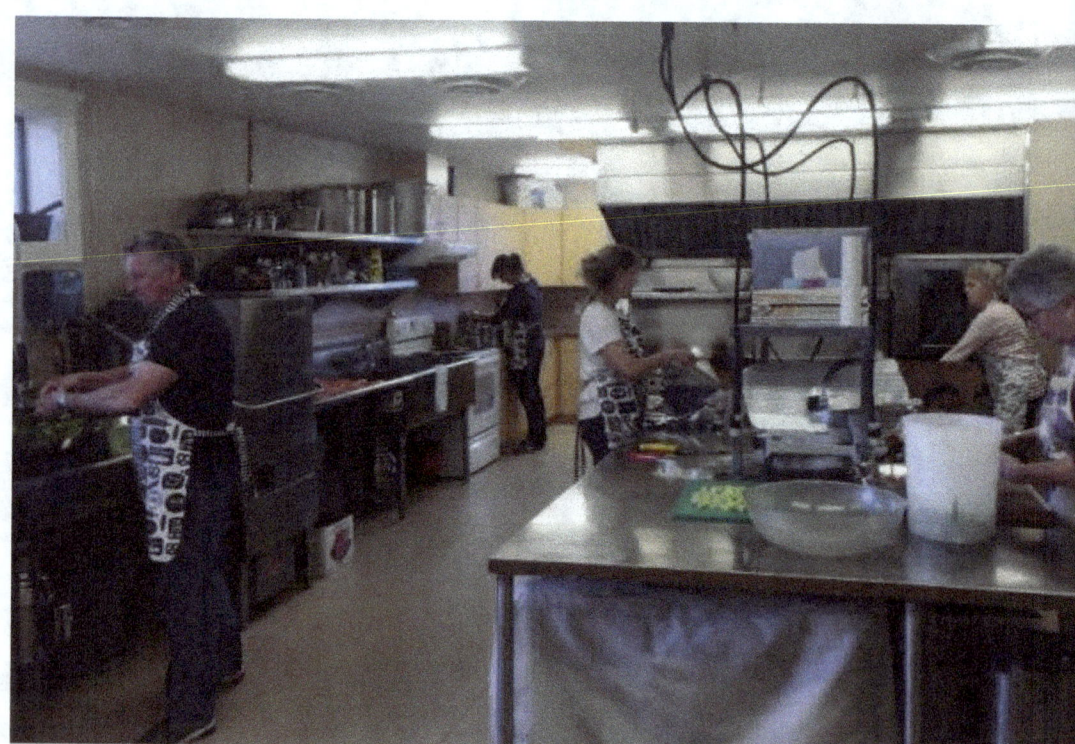

Volunteers prepare lunch in Assumption Soup Kitchen.
(2016, The Powtown Post)

The Tla'Amin Nation supported the parish' restoration of the Sacred Heart Church with a new copper roof in 2012 and restored interior in 2016. (2012, CoA)

In the early 2000s, Fr. Hamilton and Betty Wilson designed sacred vestments that honor traditional Tla'Amin culture. The eagle is both a figure of deep spiritual significance in the Tla'Amin tradition and is also the symbol of Saint John the Evangelist.

Fr. Patrick Teeporten in the restored interior of Sacred Heart Church. (2018, CoA)

The Parish Youth Group has held weekly meetings in Saint Gerard's with guest speakers or instruction in the faith, and fun events such as games, movie, crafts, and dancing. They also have floor hockey at Assumption Gym and movie night at Saint Joseph's Hall. The group has hosted neighborhood events in Wildwood such as Christmas Caroling and an outdoor Stations of the Cross on Good Friday from the church proceeding up Scout Mountain where the cross has remained planted for all to see.

Scout Mountain (2014,CoA)

The close relationship between different parish organizations and the wider community is very well demonstrated by the efforts of Assistant Pastor Irudayampattu Lazar Arockiadass, known affectionately as Father Dass. He has served the community for several years on two separate occasions, first starting in 2011.

Father Dass HGN is a member of the Heralds of Good News a Clerical Missionary Society, based in India dedicated to supplying the world with saintly priests. He has spearheaded a successful campaign along with parishioners and many non-Catholics from Powell River to set up a medical clinic in his village of Irudayampattu in an region of Southern India more than 60,000 residents without a hospital. The initiative has been a tremendous success, finding support from both Catholics and non-Catholics alike in fundraising $110,000 in order to open the clinic in spring of 2019.

On another initiative, the Assumption vegetable garden was inspired by the efforts of Assistant Pastor Father Dass, himself an elementary school teacher, both students and parishioners garden and spend time together under his care and supervision. Father Dass is loved by Assumption School students for his regular visits to the school, his sense of humor and his personal relationship with everyone in the school.

(BCC May 2, 2018)

Assistant Pastor Fr. Dass in the Assumption Parish and School Vegetable Garden.
(2014, CoA)

Archives Consulted

Archdiocese of Vancouver Archives
Archives of the Church of the Assumption
Archives of the Sisters of Charity of the Immaculate Conception
British Columbia Archives
Cortes Island Museum and Archives
Internet Archive - archive.org
Knights of Columbus Council 5417 Archives
Library and Archives Canada
Powell River Historic Museum and Archives
Sechelt Community Archives
Sunshine Coast Museum and Archives

Individuals Consulted

Adams, Leslie
Arockiadass, Father Irudayampattu Lazar, HGN
Bennett, Gerry
Bernard, Bev
Bourassa, Veronica
Bourcier, Don
Cantryn, Stephen
Clark, Patricia
Conway, Father Terry, OMI
Cossarin, Elio
Dion, Father Glenn
Gaudet, Beatrice
Gresko, Jacqueline
Hamilton, Father Bruce-John
Harry, Mary
Jablonksy, Denise
Lentz, Verna
Merlino, Elena
Paul, Dr. Elsie
Pinel, Theresa
Rigby, Evelyn
Rigby, Frank
Sapiano, Sister Claire, MSJN
Schweitzer, Frances
Sole, Rose Ann
Tepoorten, Father Patrick
Vella, Mary Lou
Vella, Sister Rose, MSJN
Waite, Ann
Wilson, Betty
Wright, Sharon

Websites Consulted

Archdiocese of Vancouver — rcav.org
Assumption School — assumptionpr.ca
The BC Catholic Paper — bccatholic.ca
Church of the Assumption — assumptionchurch.homestead.com
Faith and Light — faithandlight.org
First Voices — firstvoices.com
Knights of Columbus 5417 — kofc5417.com
Les Soeurs Missionnaires du Christ Roi — missionnairescr.org
Neh Motl Newsletter — tlaaminnation.com
Oblate Communications — omiworld.org
Powell River Living — 66.147.244.243/~prliving/wp
Powell River Peak — prpeak.com

Selected Primary Sources

A Dream that Came True. History of the Missionary Sisters of Jesus of Nazareth in Powell River. Powell River, 2011.

Chinook Manual or Prayers Hymns and Catechism in Chinook. Kamloops, 1896.

The Computer. Saint Joseph's Parish Powell River Newspaper. Vol. 1 No. 1-3, 1969.

Culos, Tony *75th Anniversary of the Powell River Italian Club.* 2012.

Duggan, J.W. *Knights of Columbus in British Columbia 1906-1986 : history in the making*, 1987.

General Financial Statement for St Joseph's Parish. Powell River, 1961.

Miller, Michael "Apology and Hope." Archdiocese of Vancouver, 2015.

«Missions Congregation des Missionaires Oblats de Marie Imaculée.» Paris, Volumes 9-40, 1868-1900.

Paul, Dr. Elsie *Written As I Remember It: Teachings from the Life of a Sliammon Elder.* Vancouver, UBC Press, 2014.

Plante, Monica SCIC "Embers from the Archives - St. Joseph's Convent Powell River, BC 1938- 1960."

Rigby, Evelyn "History of the Church of the Assumption Catholic Women's League 1935-2005." December, 2005.

"Roman Catholic Church of the Assumption Powell River." 2001.

"Roman Catholic Church of the Assumption Powell River." 2009.

"Saint Joseph's Building Fund." Powell River, BC, 1959.

"Saint Joseph's Parish Annual Report." Powell River BC, 1961.

Scicluna , Agostina "Testimonies: Sister Agostina Sicluna, M.S.J.N."

Selected Secondary Sources

Bowen, Lynne *Whoever Gives Us Bread*. Vancouver, Douglas & McIntyre, 2011.

Cluff, Alice *Powell River & District Schools 1989-1983*. Powell River, 1983.

Dawe, Helen *Helen Dawe's Sechelt*. Madeira Park, Harbour Publishing, 1990.

Cronin, Kay *Cross in the Wilderness*. Vancouver, Mitchell Press, 1959.

Gresko, Jacqueline *Traditions of Faith and Service Archdiocese of Vancouver 1908-2008*. Vancouver, Archdiocese of Vancouver, 2008.

Kennedy, Dorothy I.D. and Bouchard, Randy *Sliammon Life, Sliammon Lands*. 1983. Vancouver, Talonbooks, 1983.

Osmond, Colin Murray "Giant Trees, Iron Men: Masculinity and Colonialism in Coast Salish Loggers' Identity." U.Sask., 2016.

Southern, Karen *House histories and heritage : a visual history of the historic Powell River company townsite : Vol. 1 - the vanishing buildings*. 2013.

"Squirrel Cove." Booklet 4. Cortes Museum and Archives, 2015.

Swan, Dr. Alan *House Calls Float Plane*, Madiera Park, Harbour Publishing, 2013.

Wegner, Linda *Start Small, Dream Big The 75 Year History of BC's First Credit Union*. Victoria, First Choice Books, 2014.

Years	Oblate Missionaries Serving the Territory
1867-1868	Leon Fouquet OMI
late 1860s	Jean Marie Le Jacq OMI
late 1860s-1870s	Paul Durieu OMI
1871-1872	Charles Marchal OMI
1879-1926	Eugène Casimir Chirouse OMI
1890s	Jean-Marie-Raphaël Le Jeune, OMI
c.1901-1910, 1926-1940	Pierre Plamondon OMI
1930– c.1932	Joseph Ryder, OMI
1937, 1945-1951	Vernon Joseph Campbell OMI
1937– c.1939	James McGrath, OMI
1939	Edmund Cornell, OMI
1954– c.1957	Francis Sutherland OMI
c.1957– c.1959, 1968	Fredrick McWade OMI
1961-1965	James MacDonnell OMI
c.1967	B. MacDonald OMI

Years	Saint Joseph's Pastor	Assistant Pastor
1911	Austin Bonner	
1911-1912	Joseph McDonald	
1912-1926	Francis de Coccola	
1916-1920	Joseph B McDonald	
1920-1928	J.F. Van Wetten O.Praem	
1928-1935	Norbert Corley O.Praem	
1935-1940	Leo Hobson	
1940-1941	Lawrence Bourrie	E. McIntyre (1940)
1941-1945	Daniel McCullough OMI	Anthony McDonald (1941)
1945-1946	Anthony McDonald OMI	Forbes (1945)
1946-1947	Leo Hobson	Reidy (1946-1947)
1947-1958	Joseph McInerney	Quigley (1947-1949)
		J. Stewart (1949)
		Raymond de Coccola (1949-1954)
		Vermuelen (1954)
		Eisenring (1954-1955)
		Holzapfel (1955-1957)
		O.F. Sorel (1957-1958)
1958-1967	John Collins	Wilmer Beach (1958-1960)
		J.A. Finnigan (1960-1963)
		Roland Joncas (1963-1965)
		E. Lehner (1965-1967)
1967-1970	Joseph O'Grady	Lester Roberge (1967-1970)
		Terry Larkin (1967-1969)
		Terry Conway (1969-1970)
1970-1978	Victor Gallo	Casimir Przbylski (1970-1972)
		Thomas Nicholson (1970-1975)
		McComick (1972-1973)
		Terry Larkin (1973-1977)
		John Eason (1975-1982)

Years	Assumption Pastor	Assistant Pastor
1978-1995	Arthur Dickenson	Glenn Dion (1977-1983)
		Joseph Swoboda (1982-1984)
		Stephen Jensen (1983-1984)
		Leo Strong (1983-1984)
		Dermot McInerney (1984-1988)
		Alan Bosclair (1985-1987)
		Bruce John Hamilton (1987-1990)
		Donald Neilson (1990-1991)
		Paul Than Bui (1991-1996)
1995-2010	Bruce John Hamilton	Wilfred Gomes (1996-1999)
		Bonaventure (1997-2004)
		Tadeusz Pieniazck (1999-2000)
		Justin Trinidad (2000-2001)
		Eugenio Aloisio (2001-2003)
		Alphonse Powarth (2003-2004)
		Waldemar Podlasz (2004-2006)
		Lawrence Travis (2006-2007)
		Alan Bosclair (2007-2008)
2010-2011	Mark Schwab	Vincent Nguyen (2008-2011)
2011-2014	Edwin Neufeld	Lazar Arockiadass (2011-2016)
2014-	Patrick Tepoorten	Robert Mmegwa (2016)
		Peter Ha (2017)
		Lazar Arockiadass (2017-)

www.ingramcontent.com/pod-product-compliance
Lightning Source LLC
Chambersburg PA
CBHW050441010526
44118CB00013B/1635